Exploring Crater Lake National Park
A Family Activity Book

An educational field guide to the natural, physical, and human history of the Park.

by April Azary Thomas

Blue Lake for a Blue Planet

Oregon, known as the Beaver State,
keeps a list of its favorite things:
the hazelnut, the swallowtail butterfly,
(an insect with black and yellow wings),

> The Douglas fir tree, thunderegg rock,
> a bird—the western meadowlark,
> a fruit—the pear, and topping all its treasures
> is Crater Lake National Park.

It's a place to watch ground squirrels scramble,
slide your fingers over trunks of whitebark pine--
trees often tufted with yellow-green lichen
and brighter than candle shine.

> Indians, who first knew Mount Mazama,
> saw it explode over the plain,
> leaving walls and a deep, empty crater
> to be filled with snow-melt and rain.

The lake now holds four trillion gallons,
stretches six miles from side to side:
one sweeping glimpse of blue water
makes wonder-struck eyes open wide,

> Rainbows display the many colors
> in daylight we get from the sky;
> but Crater Lake absorbs the weaker colors,
> only blue bounces back to our eye!

by Mary Brubaker

This book is the property of

_____

Table of Contents

Table of Contents

Introduction to Crater Lake National Park

On May 22, 1902, President Theodore Roosevelt signed the bill creating Crater Lake National Park. The Lake lies inside a caldera created about 7,700 years ago, when Mount Mazama collapsed following a major eruption.

"Crater Lake National Park is located in southwest Oregon, in the Cascades Mountains. It is 22 miles long, 15 miles wide, and total area is 280 square miles - 93% terrestrial (land) and 7% aquatic (water). The park elevation ranges from 3,977' at the parks southwest boundary to 8,927" at the peak of Mount Scott." (From Terrestrial Resource Fact Sheet, Crater Lake National Park.)

Although the Park is open all year round, Rim Drive is closed during the winter months due to snow on the road. Rim Drive opens sometime between June and the middle of July depending on the amount of snow on the road. You may drive to the Rim of Crater Lake to see the Lake during the winter months. The Lodge is closed during the winter months but the Rim Visitor Center and concessions are open year round

Depending upon the time of year you visit the park, you may see a wide variety of plants and animals. Yellow monkeyflower, lupine, shooting star, or scarlet gilia are a few of the wildflowers you may see at Castle Crest Wildflower Trail. In early summer, water cascades down the cliffs at Vidae Falls while nearby you may see a frozen waterfall. In the Panhandle, you may see or hear a pair of black-backed woodpeckers searching for insects in pine or fir trees, or a chipmunk or squirrel darting up and down sugar pine trees to eat or stash pine cone seeds. A walk down Cleetwood Cove Trail to the Lake will reward you with a Lake that has gone from lapis blue to a crystal clear turquoise blue water that lets you see moss growing on the rocks a few feet below you. A trip to Wizard Island is a must. Take a hike up the cinder cone and you come to The Witches Cauldron, a crater at the top. Crater Lake National Park has a variety of habitats. Enjoy spring at the lower elevations in June and at the higher or subalpine elevations in late July. If you walk quietly or sit quietly on a log or bench you may be visited by a variety of birds and small mammals. At one of the creeks you may see an American dipper bobbing on a rock or a Belted Kingfisher diving for food. On some trails you may see a pine marten or perhaps the scat or track of a bear. Crater Lake National Park is truly a classroom with a whole new world for you to explore. **Have Fun!**

Directions to the Park. From Interstate 5, you may take Highway 62 at Medford, Highway 138 from Roseburg; Highway 97 to Highway 138 from Bend; or Highway 97 to Highway 62 from Klamath Falls.

Map of Crater Lake National Park

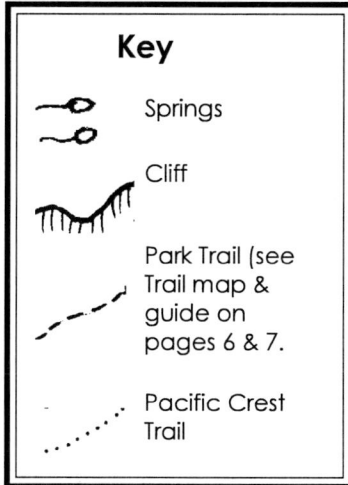

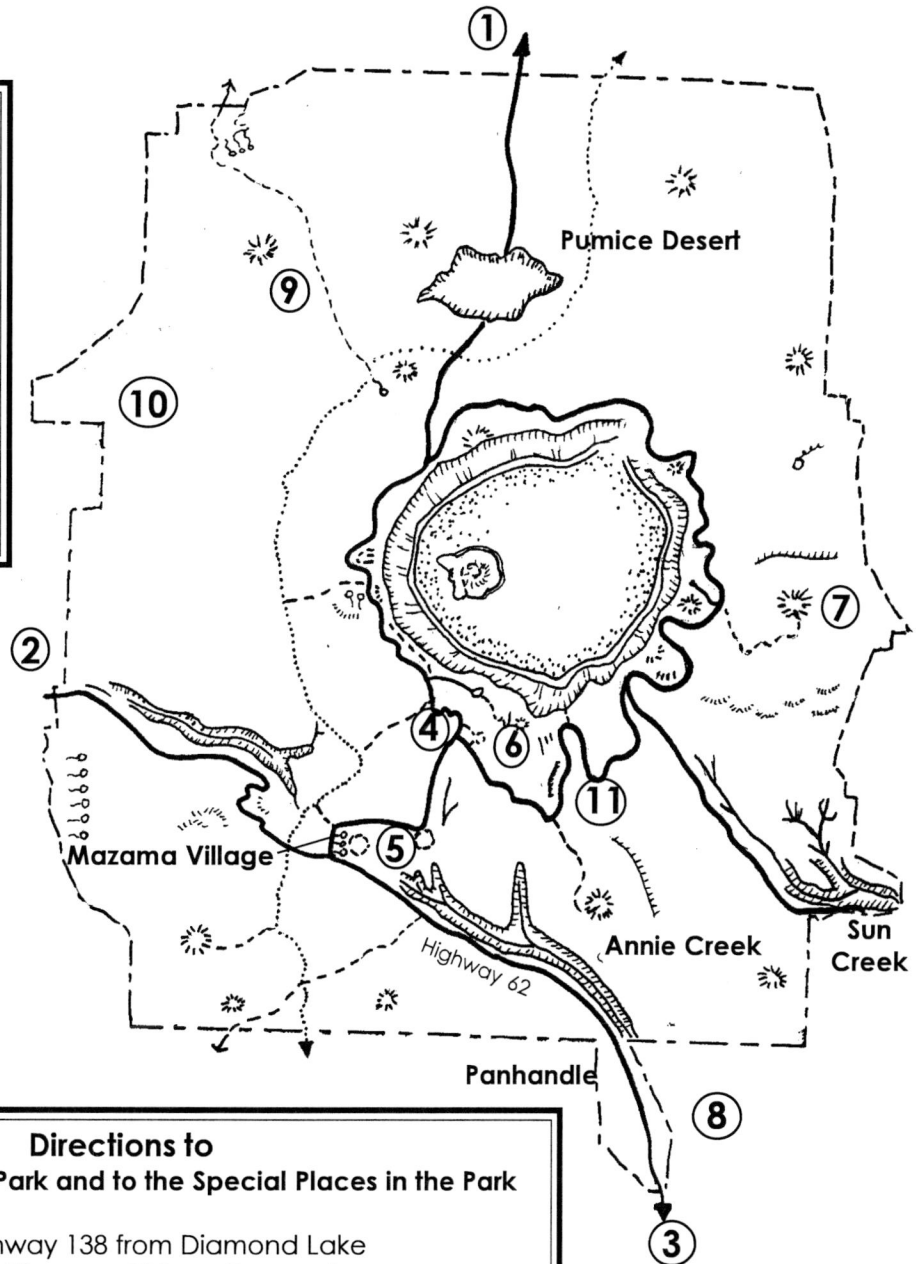

Key

- Springs
- Cliff
- Park Trail (see Trail map & guide on pages 6 & 7.
- Pacific Crest Trail

① Pumice Desert

⑨

⑩

② Mazama Village

④ ⑥

⑤

⑪

⑦ Sun Creek

Annie Creek

Highway 62

Panhandle

⑧

③

Directions to
Crater Lake National Park and to the Special Places in the Park

1 - North Entrance at Highway 138 from Diamond Lake

2 - Southwest Entrance at Highway 62 from Prospect

3 - Southeast Entrance at Highway 62 from Highway 97

4 - Steel Visitor Center & Merel S. Sager Administration Building

5 - Annie Creek - May be seen from Highway 62. Trailhead is located behind the Amphitheater at the Mazama Village Campground.

6 - Castle Crest Wildflower Trail - Can be accessed from East Rim Drive or a short walk across the hwy from the Steel Visitor Center.

7 - Mount Scott - On East Rim Drive

8 - Panhandle - Park at the Ponderosa Pine Picnic Area and walk across Hwy 62

9 - Pumice Desert - On west side of drive to North Entrance.

10 - Sphagnum Bog - Ask for directions at Steel Visitor Center.

11 - Vidae Falls - On East Rim Drive

Map of Trails

The Park has over 90 miles of trails for hikers to explore. Trails range in length from less than a mile to the 33 mile section of the Pacific Crest Trail. Trail experiences can include: climbing peaks, crossing pumice flats, strolling through forests of ponderosa pine, Shasta fir, or mountain hemlocks, or wandering along babbling streams ablaze with wildflowers. Back country trails are often old fire roads trail crews keep cleared of brush and logs.

Crater Lake National Park receives over 500 inches of snow annually. Much of the park and its trails lay under snow until late June or early July. During the winter months, hikers visit areas of the park on snow shoes or cross country skis.

Hikers should wear sturdy shoes and bring: jacket, water, food, sun screen, bug repellent, a map and compass, binoculars, **Crater Lake National Park Trails** (guide to all the trails in the park) and **Exploring Crater Lake National Park,** to help identify the plants and birds you see along the trail.

Ruffed Grouse
Bonnasa umbellus

Shooting Star
Dodecatheon alpinum

Clark's Nutcracker
Nucifraga columbia

Watchman Fire Tower

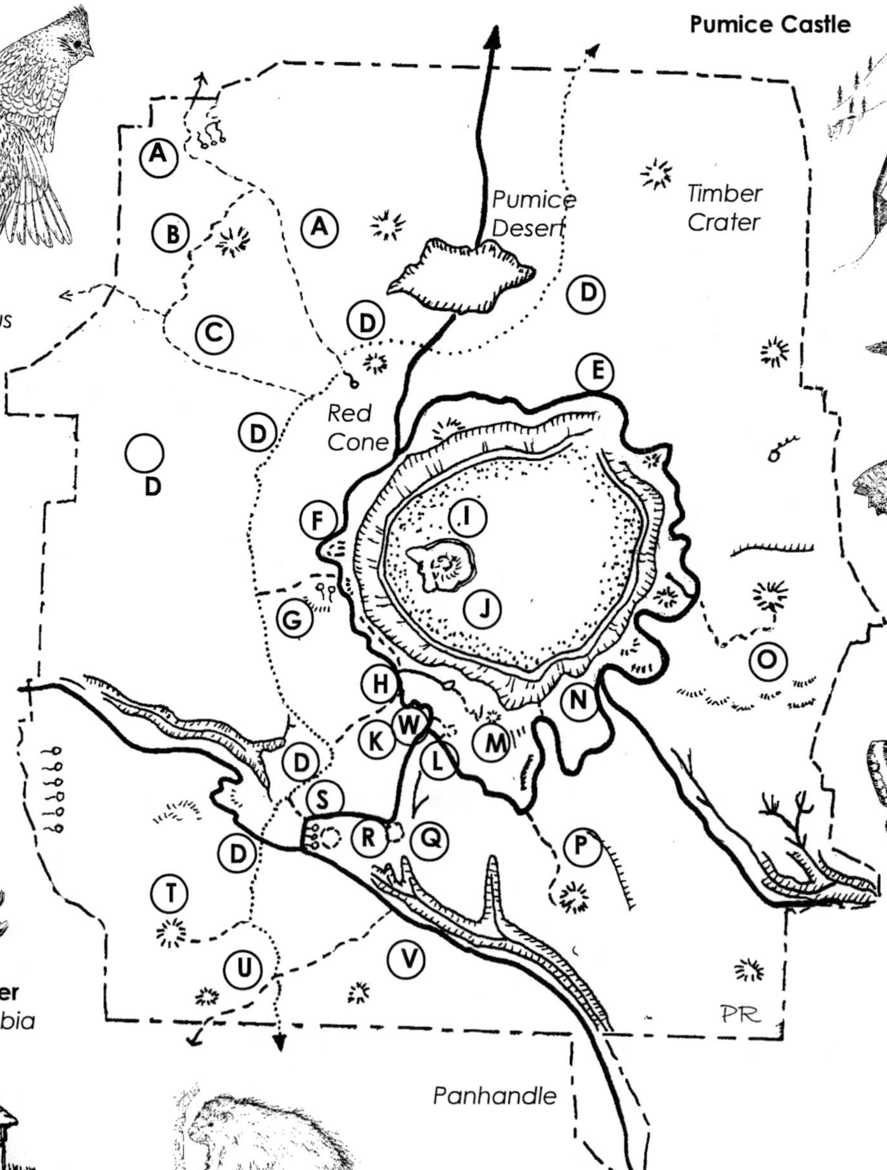

Porcupine
Erethizon dorsatum

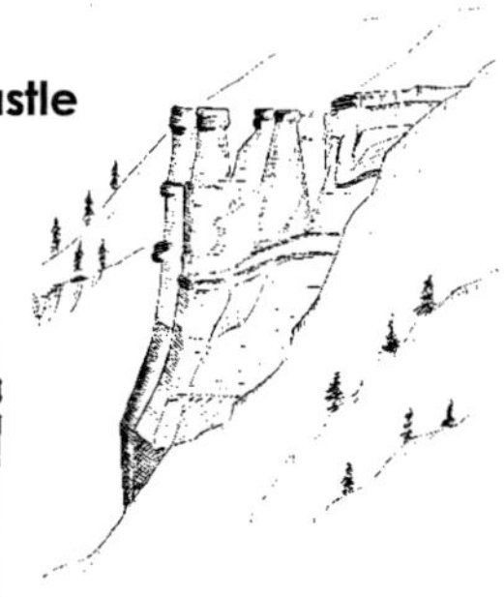

Pumice Desert

Red Cone

Pumice Castle

Timber Crater

Panhandle

PR

Lewis' Monkeyflower
Mimulus lewisii

Pandora Moth

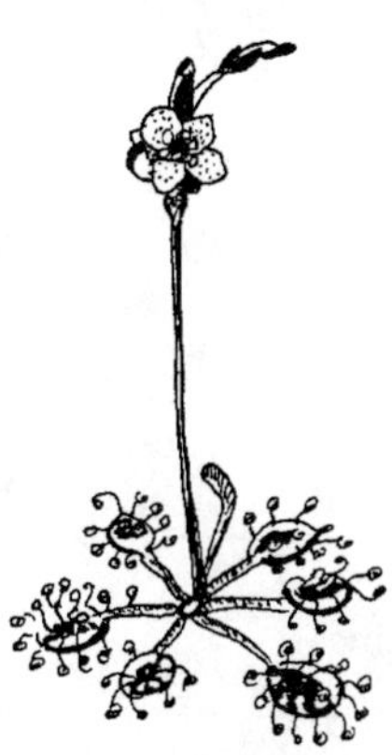

Round-leaved Sundew
Drosera roundifolia

Crater Lake Trails

Many of the Park's trails are listed below. The letter in front of the trail name is also on the map on the previous page, to help you locate the trails. Those with a *star after their names are located along Rim Drive. Descriptions of several of the trails are listed below.

Instructions: Part I - Put a ✔ on the line next to the trails you have hiked or visited.

____A -   Boundary Springs
____B -   Oasis Butte
____C -   Crater Springs
____D -   Pacific Crest
____E -   Cleetwood Cove*
____F -   Watchman Peak*
____G -   Lightning Springs*
____H -   Discovery Point
____I -   Fumarole Bay
____J -   Wizard Island Summit
____K -   Dutton Creek
____L -   Castle Crest Wildflower*

____M -   Garfield Peak
____N -   Sun Notch Trailhead*
____O -   Mount Scott*
____P -   Crater Peak
____Q -   Godfrey Glen
____R -   Annie Creek
____S -   Annie Springs Cutoff
____T -   Union Peak
____U -   Stuart Falls
____V -   Pumice Flats
____W -   Lady of the Woods (formerly called Park Headquarters Historic Walking Tour)

☙Castle Crest Wildflower Trail is a short ¼ mile loop through a forest. A meadow and streams flow down from the cliff; in June and July this area is ablaze with wildflowers. The Castle Crest Wildflower Trail section on page 70 lists some of the plants and animals you may see while visiting the trail. A self-guiding brochure is available at the trailhead.

☙Godfrey Glen Trail is a one mile loop. As you walk the trail through a forest of mountain hemlocks and Shasta red firs look for a waterfall, pumice pinnacles, and a variety of songbirds, deer, and squirrels. A self-guided brochure is available at the trailhead.

☙Mount Scott Trail is approximately 5 miles round trip to the summit. This mountain is a cinder cone that was on the flank of Mount Mazama. A steep trail crosses pumice and stands of whitebark pine. For more information about Mount Scott refer to page 80 of this book.

☙Watchman Peak Trail is a mile and a half round trip to the summit and is moderately steep. There is very little vegetation along the trail. Pikas and squirrels may be seen, and it is a good place to watch for falcons, hawks, and eagles during spring and fall migration.

Part II - Draw a picture of a plant, animal, or feature you saw on your favorite trail.

Crater Lake Trails

While out on the trail you may not see any of the animals listed below, but they are there. One way to tell which animals live in or visit the trail is to look for their *signs*. *Signs* may be a feather, animal track, scat, or bear scratch marks on a tree. Refer to *Key to Mammal Tracks* on page 37, or *Mammal Field Guide* on pages 38 and 39. For birds, refer to pages 41 through 47.

Instructions: Hidden in the puzzle below are some of the names of animals you may see on the trails in the park. The words can be found forward, backwards, up, down, or diagonally. Circle the letters of the words as you find them in the puzzle. Write the uncircled letters on the line below. The uncircled letters spell out the names of trees commonly seen on the trails.

_____

Bear
Beetle
Bull Trout
Chickadee
Chickaree
Coyote
Deer
Elk

Hawk
Jay
Lizard
Marmot
Mice
Owl
Pika

Pine Marten
Porcupine
Red Fox
Shrew
Songbird
Squirrel
Vole
Woodpecker

Bull Trout
Salvelinus confluenteus

American (Pine) Marten
Martes americana

**American (Pine)
Marten Tracks**

```
P X K W A H K D E E R M O
I O W L U L E L T E E B N
N F R T E E R A K C I H C
E D P C A M I C E Y S I H
M E M I U N E H A Q O E I
A R A E K P M J U E N D C
R A R L D A I I L T G R K
T E M O O C R N K O B A A
E B O V & R F I E Y I Z D
N W T W E R H S R O R I E
B U L L T R O U T C D L E
```

Beetle

Mountain Hemlock
Tsuga mertensiana

American Pika
Ochotona princeps

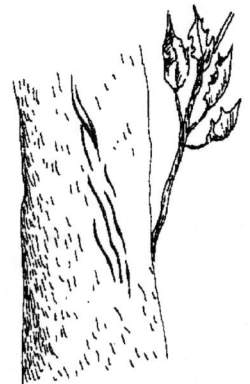

**Animal Sign - Bear
Claw Marks on
Tree.**

Animal Sign - Owl Pellet

Geology

The speckled area on the map shows the approximate extent of the ash fall of Mount Mazama when it erupted 7,700 years ago. The ash fall was 500 times that of Mount St. Helens in 1980. 5,000 square miles of ash was distributed over 6 states and 3 Canadian Provinces.

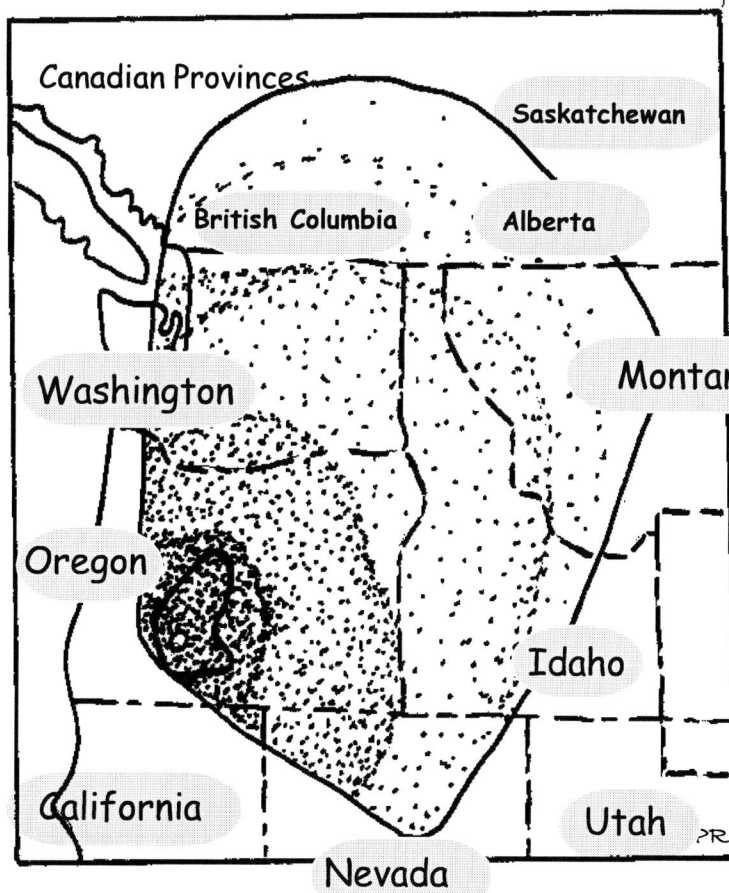

Canadian Provinces
Saskatchewan
British Columbia
Alberta
Washington
Montana
Oregon
Idaho
California
Utah
Nevada

Eruption and Collapse of Mount Mazama

Mount Mazama is part of the new Cascade Mountain Range that extends from Mt. Lassen Volcano (Lassen Volcanic National Park) all the way north to Mount Garibaldi in British Columbia. There are over 15 active or dormat volcanoes in the range. Ages of the volcanoes vary from 30,000 years old to over 3 million. The large caldera occupied by Crater Lake and the encircling flanks and ridges are all that is left of once-mighty Mount Mazama. Mazama's early history was similar to that of the other composite cones of the Cascades. From its foundation rocks at the base (between 5,000 and 6,000 feet in elevation), Mount Mazama rose another 6,000 feet to an elevation of approximately 10,000 to 12,000 feet above sea level. The cone was broader and less steep than Shasta's or Rainier's because the lateral vents and overlapping cones gave the volcano a bulky, irregular shape. After the collapse, the caldera remained hot with continuing eruptions. Merriam Cone is the result of these smaller eruptions, as is Wizard Island. Cracks within the caldera may have prevented water from accumulating in the caldera for many centuries. There are still thermal springs at the bottom of Crater Lake, which host a variety of aquatic invertebrates and mosses.

Instructions: Listed below are the descriptions of the eruption of Mount Mazama. Words in **bold** are in the puzzle below. The first letter of several of the words has been provided to start you out.

Mount Mazama grew over hundreds of thousands of years with many small eruptions. Magma rose to the top of the **volcano** through the central and lateral **vent**s. (See illustration on page 12)

Mount Mazama begins its destructive eruptions about 7,700 years ago. The **eruption** was about 40 times the size of Mount St. Helen's eruption in 1980. The diagram on page 9 shows how far away ash fell.

As eruptions become more violent, the crater enlarges and dacite **ash** and **pumice** are ejected and blown over the region.

Collapse of the cone and its magma chamber creates a large **caldera**, five miles wide and 4,000 feet deep. More volcanic material falls back into the caldera than flows out or is blown away during the weaker explosive eruptions that continue for a number of years.

Subsequent smaller eruptions form **Wizard Island** and partially fill the caldera, smoothing the basin floor. **Rain**water, **snow**melt, and surface runoff gradually filled the caldera, creating Crater Lake over a period of about 300 years.

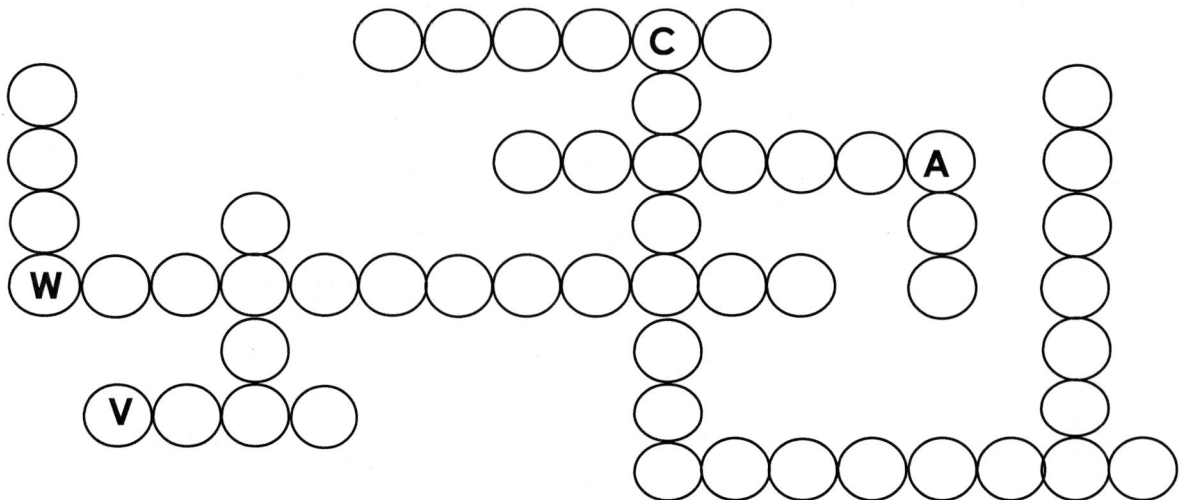

Eruption and Collapse of Mount Mazama

Instructions: Illustrated below are the sequences of the eruption of Mount Mazama. On the previous page are descriptions of each stage of the eruption. On the line below each illustration, write a 2 to 5 word description of each event. An example has been provided.

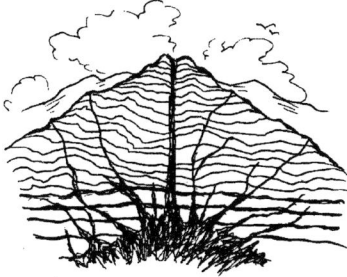

Slow growth of Mount Mazama.

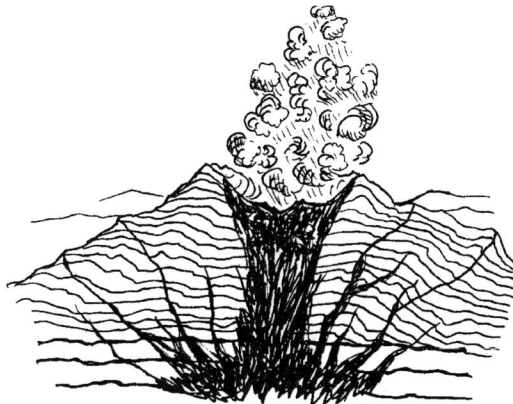

_____   _____

_____   _____

_____

Geology

About 25 percent of the earth's surface is igneous in origin. Volcanic rocks are igneous rocks formed by the extrusion of magma (hot molten materials inside the earth) to the surface. The sea floor and some mountains were formed by countless eruptions. A volcano is a place on the Earth's surface where molten rock, gases, and pyroclastic debris (ash, pumice, & other rocks) erupt through the earth's crust. Volcanoes vary quite a bit in their structure - some are cracks in the earth's crust where lava erupts, and some are domes, shields, or mountain-like structures with a crater at the summit. Gaseous emissions from volcanoes formed the earth's atmosphere. There are more than 500 active volcanoes in the world. More than half of these volcanoes are part of the "Ring of Fire," a region encircling the Pacific Ocean.

Most of the volcanoes in the Cascades are considered "composite" or "stratovolcanoes," because they have alternating layers of lava and volcanic debris. They tend to explode when they erupt, causing a lot of damage. The Cascade Mountain range of volcanoes is thought to be approximately 30,000 years old to about seven million years old. Mount St. Helens and Mount Baker in Washington state are the youngest of the principle volcanoes, being about 30,000 to 50,000 years old.

Instructions: The drawing below illustrates the different layers of ash and lava. Color the layers of the volcano. Color the ash layers grey and the lava layers red.

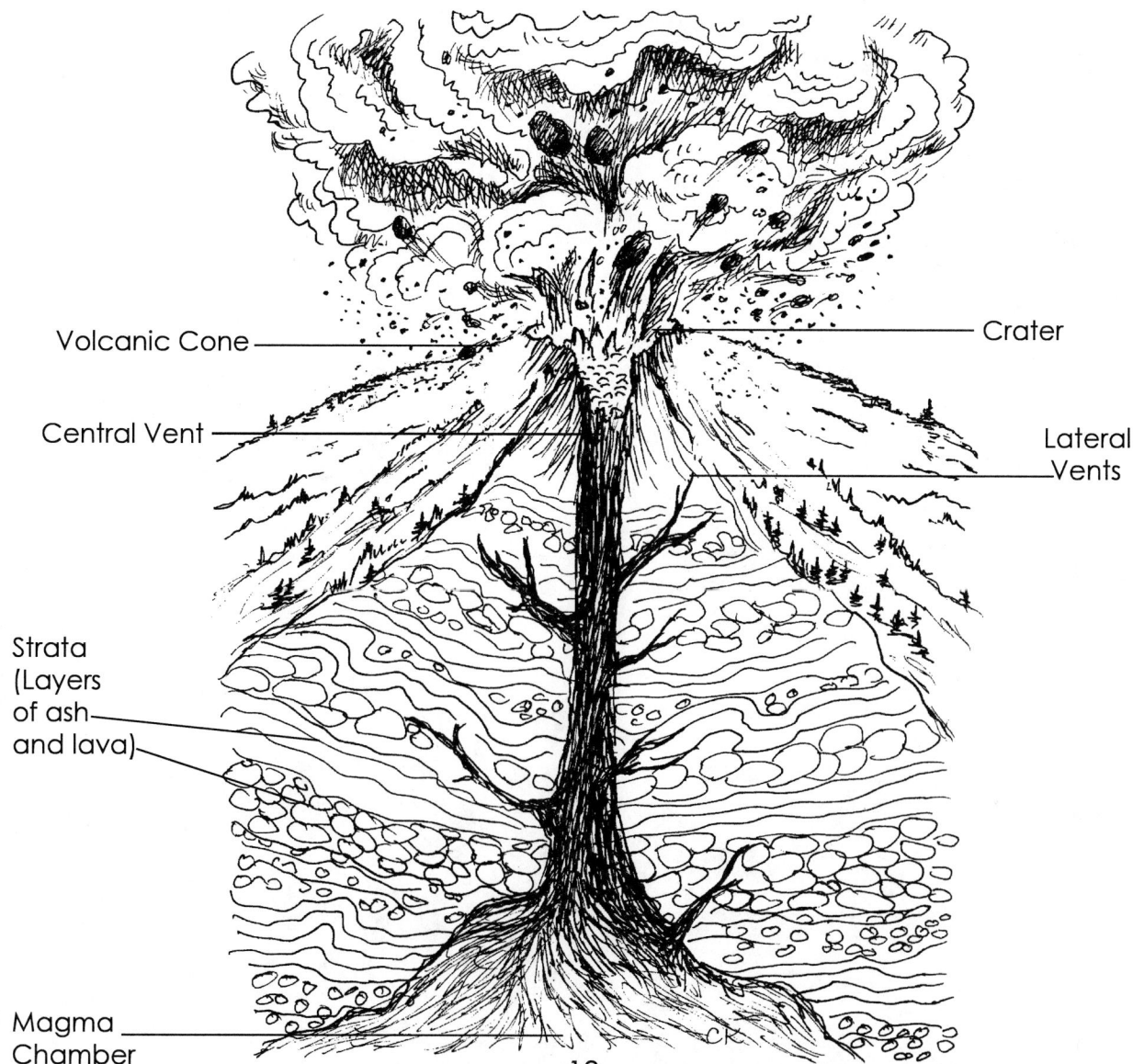

Volcanic Cone

Central Vent

Crater

Lateral Vents

Strata (Layers of ash and lava)

Magma Chamber

Mount Mazama Word Search

In the puzzle below are words associated with Mount Mazama and Crater Lake. Words listed below can be found backwards, forward, up, down, or diagonally. Words in parenthesis are not included in the puzzle. Circle the letters of the words. Write the uncircled letters on the line below. The uncircled letters spell out the names of two geologic features found in the lake.

Ash
Blast
Caldera
Cascade Range
Cinders
Composite
Cone
Crack
Crater
Dormant
Earthquake
Eruption
Flow
Gas
Lateral Vent
Lava
Magma Chamber
Molten Rock
Phantom (Ship)
Pumice
Strata
Volcano
Wizard (Island)

```
              A V A L
            P U M I C E
          N O I T P U R E
        M A G M A C H A M B E R
    F L O W C A S C A D E R A N G E
    M C L E R I R A O R I S R M M T
    O A T A A N N R G C H R T O D I
    N L E O C N M D A E , B H T R S
    A D N G K A E T E T O L Q N A O
    C E R T N H A E A R R A U A Z P
    L R O T M R A R L V S S A H I M
    O A C E T N C O N E T T K P W O
    V S K S L A T E R A L V E N T C
```

CK

-13-

Geological Features of the Caldera

Llao Rock

Llao Rock is obsidian, a glassy dacite dome, a layer of pumice rich in silica, covered by a lava flow from the eruption of Mount Mazama on the caldera rim. It was formed hundreds of years before the eruption of Mount Mazama. Glacial striations and glacial polish, marks made by the forward and retreating glaciers up to a thousand feet thick, can be found on Llao Rock. Llao Rock is a good place to see the gray-crowned rosy finch, Newberry knotweed, Lyall lupine, spreading phlox, pussypaws, pumice grapefern, and grasses and sedges.

Devil's Backbone

The Devil's Backbone is a vertical wall, an andesitic (a fine-grained gray volcanic rock) dike, which runs up the cliffs of Crater Lake, from the water's edge to the west rim. It is called the Devil's Backbone because it resembles a backbone. A dike is formed when magma pushes up through the mountain and breaks through the horizontal rock layers with or without reaching the surface. The Devil's Backbone is approximately 1,000' long and 50' across near the top. On some rocks glacial striations and polish can be found. Phantom Ship is also a dike, a remnant of a volcano that erupted perhaps as long ago as 400,000 years.

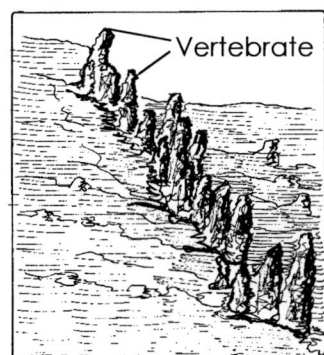

Vertebrate

Pumice Castle

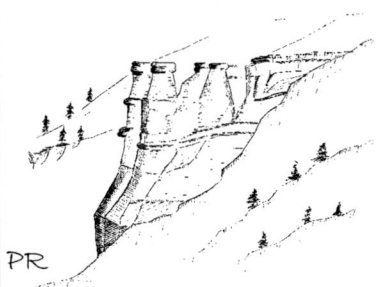

Pumice Castle, also called Red Castle or Castle Rock, is made of ash from the Mount Mazama eruption 7,700 years ago. The ash has been eroded away by water and wind, leaving the pinkish-brown andesite turrets, which resemble a "castle." Pumice Castle is located on the East Rim Drive.

The Pinnacles

Pinnacles can be found along Wheeler Creek Canyon, Castle Creek Canyon, and Annie Creek Canyon. Pinnacles are remnants of ash flows, and are hollow as the result of escaping gases. As the lava flows from Mount Mazama filled glacial valleys with buff-colored rhyodacite pumice, vents formed and hot gases escaped. As Mount Mazama continued to erupt, a darker andesite scoria catapulted into "glowing" avalanches and covered the earlier flows. This was followed by a final flow of brownish ash. As the vents cooled, the escaping gases cemented the loose pumice. Wind, rain, and sleet over the last 6,000 years have eroded away the softer materials of pumice and scoria, leaving hollow fossil fumeroles, gas vents, or spires. As you walk along Annie Creek or Godfrey Glen Trails, look to see if any birds are sitting on a pinnacle. Sit quietly along the trail and listen for their song. Then look for them on the pinnacles. **Please note, there are no trails leading to the Pinnacles, the ground is unstable and hazardous to walk on.**

Other Geological Features of the Park

As you drive along Rim Drive, walk the Rim Trail, take a ride on the lake in a tour boat*, or explore other parts of the park, there are many more geological features you may see. In addition to Llao Rock, Devil's Backbone, and Pumice Castle, Phantom Ship is illustrated on pages 16 and 17, and the Pumice Desert may be found on pages 84 and 85.

Instructions: In the checklist below, place a ✔ next to each geological feature you see in the Park. Below or on your journal pages at the back of the book, write down what you saw and what you found interesting. Where there trees there or did you see a bird or animal?

View from one of several caves in the walls of the caldera.

_____	Applegate Peak
_____	Ash
_____	Cave
_____	Garfield Peak
_____	Glacial Polish
_____	Grotto Cove
_____	Hillman Peak
_____	Lady in the Lake
_____	Lava
_____	Merriam Cone
_____	Pumice Desert
_____	Red Cone
_____	Skell Head
_____	Sun Notch
_____	Thermal Vent
_____	Union Peak

The Pumice Desert is covered with thousands of pieces of pumice.

Lady of the Lake sits in front of Grotto Cove.

The Notch

Sun Notch, from Reflection Point

_____

_____

_____

_____

_____

*Tours on Crater Lake can be reached by buying tickets for the tour boat at Cleetwood Cove, then hiking down the Cleetwood Cove trail.

Phantom Ship

From various locations on the Rim of Crater Lake, you can see what appears to be a ship in the water. You may see falcons, hawks, eagles, gulls, and other birds perched on one of the trees or perhaps a swallow flying into a crevice in the "ship" to feed its chicks. What you are looking at is not a ship, but a remnant of a former volcano.

As with many volcanoes, Mount Mazama grew to its 12,000 feet as the result of multiple earlier eruptions. **Phantom Ship** is a remnant of one of those eruptions and all that is left today is a dike, a channel through which magma pushed its way up through the volcano and caused breaks in rock layers above it. Phantom Ship is made up of andesite lava flows associated with the 400,000 year old Phantom Cone. Phantom Ship is a small island with triangular "sails" that rises more than 160 feet above the water and is over 300 feet long, close to the lakeshore on the southeast side. Phantom Ship is the oldest rock within the caldera and has eroded to its present shape. Seven species of trees grow on the island, and birds visit and nest there.

Depending upon the sunlight, sometimes Phantom Ship appears to disappear into the face of Dutton Ridge, hence it was called a "phantom" ship.

Phantom Ship as seen from the tour boat.

Phantom Ship

Although a large volcanic island in the middle of Crater Lake, Phantom Ship hosts a variety of plants and birds. As Phantom Ship eroded away, wind and birds brought seeds from the forest trees. These seeds sprouted and today trees and birds live on the "Ship." Seven species of trees grow on the island, violet-green and green swallows nest in the cavities that resulted from erosion over thousands of years. Other birds seen on the "Ship" include bald eagles, gray jays, and Clark's nutcracker.

Instructions: Match the trees and birds with their name. Write the # of the tree or bird on the line near each picture. Color the plants and animals, then color the name of the plant or animal the same color. **Hint**: The scientific names for all trees and birds are listed. To find their common names, you may look them up on the bird and tree checklists on pages 41 and 56.

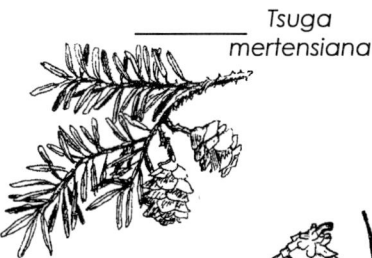

_____ *Tsuga mertensiana*

Abies magnifica shastensis

_____

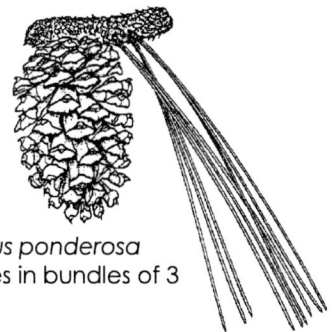

Pinus ponderosa
Needles in bundles of 3

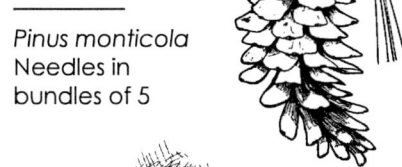

_____
Pinus monticola
Needles in bundles of 5

1) Bald Eagle

2) Gray Jay

3) Shasta Red Fir

4) Mountain Hemlock

5) Subalpine Fir

6) Western White Pine

7) Ponderosa Pine

8) Whitebark Pine

9) Lodgepole Pine

10) Clark's Nutcracker

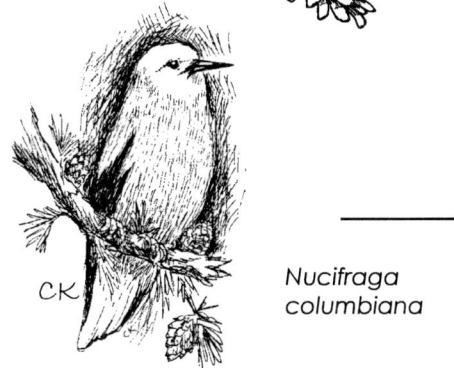

_____
Nucifraga columbiana

_____
Perisoreus canadensis

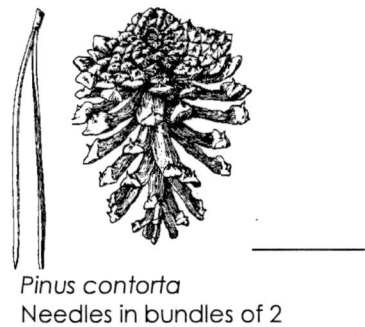

_____
Pinus contorta
Needles in bundles of 2

Pinus albicaulis
Needles in bundles of 5

_____

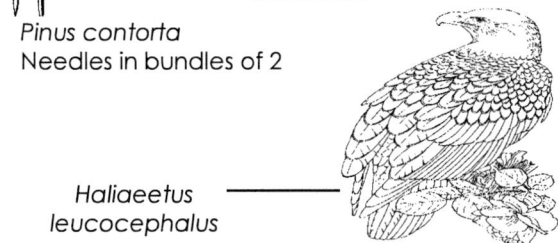

Haliaeetus leucocephalus _____

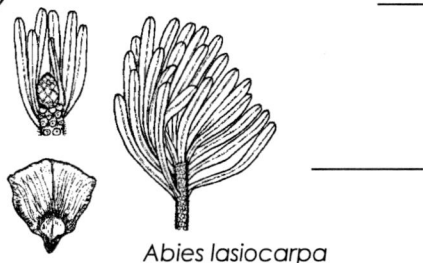

_____
Abies lasiocarpa

Wizard Island

Whether you stand at Discovery Point or anywhere along Rim Drive, Wizard Island looks like a perfect cinder cone (a steep-sided, symmetrical cone, formed by the eruption of cinders, ash, and other pyroclastic materials). As you walk up the trail to the top of Wizard Island, you can see that instead of erupting from the top of the cone, the lava flowed out of a fissure on the side of the cone, a very large crater is at the top, over 100 feet deep. William G. Steel, on August 17, 1885, named this crater "The Witches Cauldron." Inside the cauldron, the area is littered with downed logs.

Be sure to take the boat ride and allow time to explore the many treasures of Wizard Island. Look at the crystal clear, turquoise blue water at Fumerole Bay. You will see moss covered boulders, and maybe fish. As you color this illustration of Wizard Island, add in plants and animals. Some are listed in the puzzles on the pages 20 and 21.

Wizard Island rises 774 feet above the surface of the water, and the summit is 6,933 feet above sea level. The Witches Cauldron is 100' deep and 300' wide.

Wizard Island: Succession of Life

Cataclysmic events take place all over the world - fire, volcanic eruptions, earthquakes, floods, and hurricanes. Out of each disturbance, from the rubble left of an eruption or the burnt forest, comes new life.

Standing on the rim of the caldera, you may see evidence of "succession of life" - the beginnings of new life on the young volcano. The Island is composed of andesitic lava at the base, with ash and cinders on the slopes and the top. This makes it hard for plants to take hold and grow, although hemlock, pine, and firs can be found growing here, even in the crater.

Soon after the eruption of Mount Mazama wind brought spores of rock lichens. Lichen (algae & fungi living in a mutualist symbiotic relationship) live on boulders, cliffs, rocks, and trees. They can survive the harsh winters at Crater Lake and grow 1/25 to ½" a year. The lichens are able to decompose enough rock material by their secretions to gain a foothold. As you walk around Wizard Island, notice the grey, green, red, orange, brown, or yellow lichens growing on rocks. While walking in the forests you may see tree lichens hanging down branches of conifers and hardwoods. When the lichen die they contribute minute amounts of organic material. After a sufficient amount of soil collects, moss arrives. In time, after the mosses, hearty wildflowers arrive.

Wind and birds bring a variety of winged and hitchhiker seeds (seeds with spikes or barbs) that may or may not adapt to living in this harsh environment of Wizard Island. Those seeds that do succeed and grow have adapted to life on the Island. In addition to lichen, you may see lace fern growing on lower rock ledges.

As plants continue to increase in numbers, so will the number of animals who live on the Island. Dragonflies attract toads, wildflowers and insects attract red-breasted nuthatches, hummingbirds, and juncos, and golden-mantled ground squirrels come to eat seeds of the whitebark pine trees.

A Wizard Island "Succession of Life" and a Wizard Island food web would be:

Succession of LIfe: Lava -> lichens -> moss -> vascular plants
Food Web: Vascular plants -> insects -> reptiles & amphibians -> birds -> mammals.

It may take hundreds or thousands of years for more soil to form to host a larger variety of plants. Wizard Island, as it is, is one of the "Jewels of the Park."

Be sure to visit and appreciate the struggle for life in this difficult environment. It is truly remarkable, from Skell Channel to Fumerole Bay to the bottom of "Witches Cauldron" at the top of Wizard Island. The environment is constantly changing. On your next visit record any changes that you notice that have taken place on Wizard Island.

Plants of Wizard Island

Plant life on the Island is sparse. The island is volcanic in nature and does not have suitable soil for many plants to grow in. There are several species of trees - primarily western hemlock at the lower elevations and whitebark pine at the higher elevations. A few birds and mammals visit the island and some birds such as dark-eyed junco's nest on Wizard Island.

Instructions: Below are some of the plants you may see on Wizard Island. Words in **bold** type are in the puzzle below. Several letters have been placed in the puzzle to get you started.

Mountain **Hemlock**
Tsuga mertensiana

Brewer's **Sedge**
Carex brewerii

Fireweed
Epilobium angustifolium
Flowers: Deep pink to magenta

Heartleaf Arnica
Arnica cordifolia
Flowers: Yellow

Lace Fern
Cheilanthes gracillima

Lodgepole **Pine**
Pinus contorta murrayana
Needles in bundles of 2
Cones: 1 ½" - 2" long

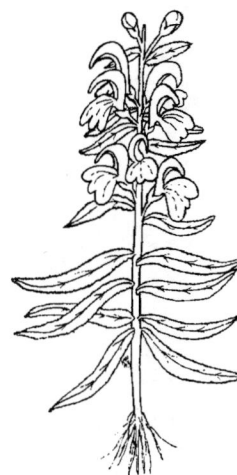

Red-fruited Elder
Sambucus racemosa callicarpa

Parrot's Beak or
Sickleleaf Lousewort
Pedicularis racemosa
Flowers: Pale pink, purple, or white

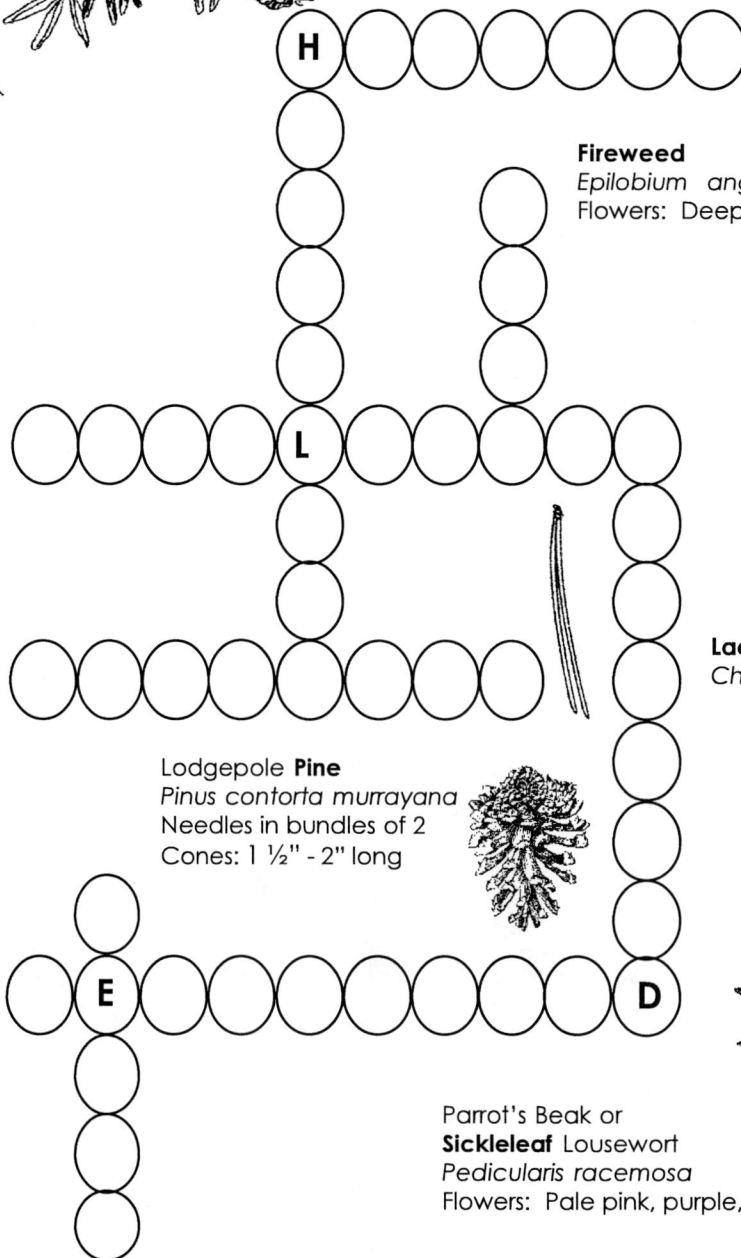

Animals of Wizard Island

How did the animals arrive on the island? Some of the smaller ones may have "stowed" away on a boat. Others may swim across Skell Channel, which is the shallowest point between the shoreline and the island. And others may fly, such as the dark-eyed junco who nests on the Island.

Instructions: Below are some of the animals you may see on Wizard Island. Use the words in **bold** type to fill in the blanks below. Letters in the squares (reading down) will spell out the name of another animal you may see on Wizard Island. Several letters have been placed in the puzzle to get you started. The name of the animal is _____.

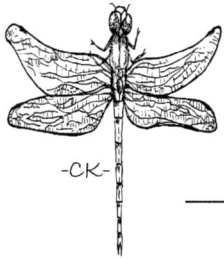

__ __ __ __ [L] __ __ __

__ __ __ __ [ ] __ __ __

__ __ __ [ ] M __ __ __

__ __ __ [ ] __ __ __

__ __ __ P __ [ ] __ __

[F] __ __ __ __ __

__ __ __ [ ] __ __ __

__ __ __ [ ] __ __ __

__ __ __ [ ] F __ __

Dragonfly
-CK-

Peregrine **Falcon**
Falco peregrinus

Garter Snake
Thamnophis sirtailis
-CK-

Golden-crowned **Kinglet**
Regulus satrapa

Golden-mantled Ground **Squirrel**
Spermophiluis lateralis
-CK-

Deer Mouse
Peromyscus maniculatus

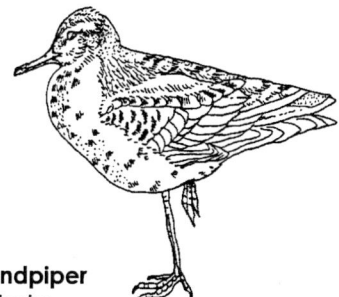

Mule Deer
Odocolleus hemionus
N.P. IMHOF

Townsend's **Chipmunk**
Tamias townsendii

Spotted Sandpiper
Actitis solitaria

-21-

Crater Lake Winters

Winters at Crater Lake can be very harsh for staff, visitors, and the plants and animals that live in the park. Annually, Crater Lake National Park averages about 500" of snow. The snow is important for the lake, and for the residents of the surrounding areas. The snow melt fills the lake, creeks, and rivers, and brings much needed water to the valleys.

The park is especially beautiful after a snow storm. The trees are covered in snow and snow crystals shimmer when the sun breaks through the clouds. Driving, though, can be a problem, and if you visit the Park in the winter to snowshoe or cross-country ski, be sure to bring along tire chains for your vehicle. Snow tires and/or a 4-wheel drive vehicle navigate the snow pack easier.

All winter long, snow crews plow the roads leading into the park from the south entrance on Highway 62 and the road to the Rim. Some days it can take a very long time to go a short distance. After the snow plow pushes the fresh snow to the side of the road, the rotary snow plow follows and blows the snow up over the snow bank and into the woords/forest. After a major storm, snow crews may work from 4:00 a.m. to 8:00 pm to open up Highway 62 and park roads so staff can come to work or drive home. If you look carefully at the rotary snow plow you will see that the tires look like ribbons.

Drive to the Rim near the Lodge, and look out at the Lake. Although East and West Rim Drives are closed in the winter, it is well worth the drive up. Snow pack can be 20 to 30 feet tall! Opening the Rim Drive by June or the first week of July is a major undertaking. Clearing 2/10 mile of roadway per day, it takes about 3 ½ months to clear all of Rim Drive. When West Rim Drive is cleared, the north entrance is opened, while the snow crew continue working on the remainder of Rim Drive.

Instructions: **Part I -** Below is a rotary snow plow. It follows behind the push plow and blows snow out of the roadway. The "ribbon" tires spin at a high rpm and feed snow into a large fan behind the ribbons. The fan blows the snow out a chute approximately 125 feet off the roadway. Color the snow equipment yellow and the rotary snow plow tires (ribbons) black. Do you think it would be fun to sit in the driver's seat? You have a great view of the road, if you can see it. **Part II -** On the next page is a weather report provided by the National Park Service and the Department of Interior. The charts show: month-by-month snow and precipitation accumulations for 2006/2007, the maximun and minimum snow levels, and accumulated daily snowfall. In the box below, keep records of the amount of snow you receive at your home.

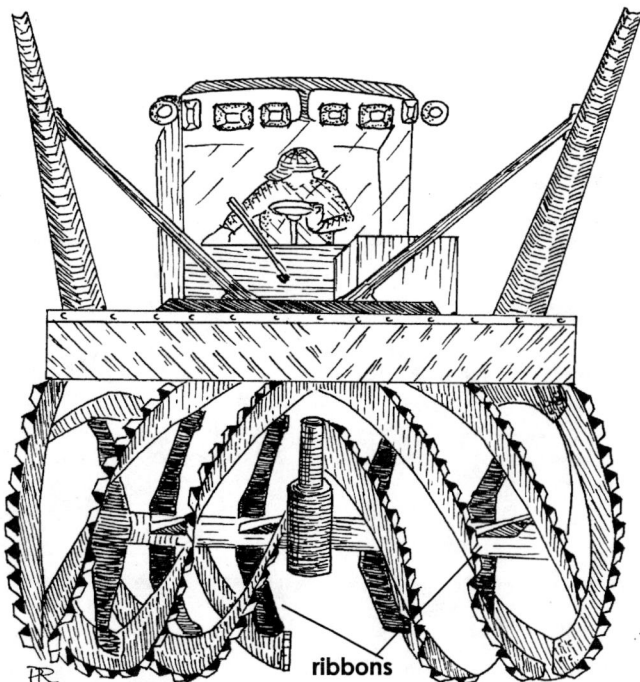

The rotary snow plow is one of the vehicles used to clear the snow and ice off the roads of Crater Lake National Park.

ribbons

My Snow Report

25"
20"
15"
10"
5"
0"

6'

Nov Dec Jan Feb Mar April

CRATER LAKE REPORT 05/15/2007

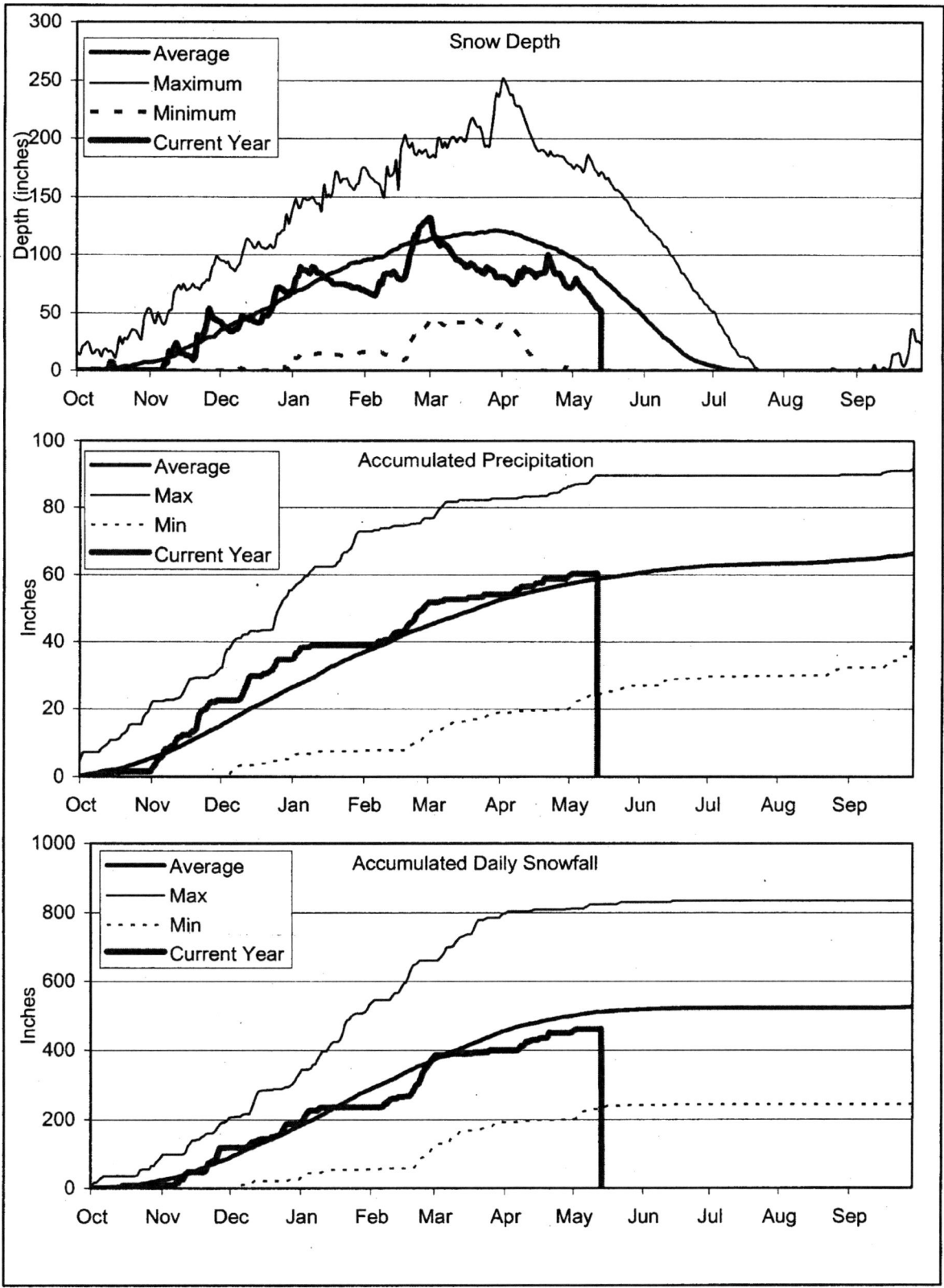

Snow Depth

Accumulated Precipitation

Accumulated Daily Snowfall

Sinnott Memorial Overlook

CK

CK

The Watchman Lookout was built in 1931

History

History of Crater Lake Puzzle

Instructions: In the puzzle below are some of the words associated with the history of Mount Mazama and Crater Lake National Park. Words in **bold** are found in the puzzle. The first letter of several words have been provided to start you out.

Peter **Britt**
Captain Clarence **Dutton**
Chief Llao
Chief **Skell**
Cleetwood
Crater Lake **Lodge**
Creation Story
Deep Blue Lake
Fish

Fred H. **Kiser**
KlamathTribes
James M. **Sutton**
John Wellesey **Hillman**
Lake **Majesty**
Merel S. **Sager**
Molala Tribe

National **Park**
Native Peoples
Sacred **Place**
Storytelling
William Gladstone **Steel**

Kokanee Salmon

Klamath Tribe member at Crater Lake

NPS   Crater Lake Lodge

Sandals and other artifacts found buried under ash from the Mount Mazama eruption 7,700 years ago.

William Gladstone Steel and friends lowering Steel's boat into Crater Lake.

Native Peoples

Long before white people discovered Crater Lake, Native People regarded Mount Mazama, and then Crater Lake, as a sacred place. The closest tribe was the Molala, who lived on the slopes of the Cascade Mountain range. They hunted and gathered throughout the area. The Klamath Tribe thought the mountain sacred and visited Mount Mazama and eventually Crater Lake on spiritual or vision quests. The Upper Umpqua, the Takelma, Shasta, Modoc, and/or several Paiute bands may also have visited what is now called Crater Lake National Park.

Storytelling

For thousands of years during the winter months local Native American tribes sat around the fire at night and told stories of their ancestors and the way they lived. Legends and tribe folklore were passed from one generation to the next by telling stories. Storytelling was a very important way of teaching children about a tribe's history, religion, and culture.

As the fur traders, explorers, gold miners, and settlers moved west, tribes were moved to reservations, where they were made to adapt to the ways of white Americans. They were prohibited from speaking their native language or practicing their religion, or crafts, or dress in tribal clothing. One of the ways tribes kept their culture and history alive was through storytelling. Because of storytelling, some of the tribal customs have been saved and are again being practiced by tribe and non-tribal members.

Instructions: Below is a retelling of a creation story by Mindy Dwyer about how Crater Lake came to be. Read the story and then in the box below, draw a picture to go with the story.

A long, long time ago, Coyote had magical powers. The Great One asked Coyote to do many things for him. Like Raven, he liked shiny things. UP in the sky one night Coyote saw a blue star and immediately fell in love with her. Coyote was in LOVE with her. He watched her each night and his eyes followed her as she crossed the sky, from east to west. As the stars passed over the peak of Mount Mazama, it appeared to touch the star. The next night he ran up Mount Mazama and waited for her to appear. As she appeared, he noticed he still could not touch her. "Blue Star," Coyote called to her. "Will you be my wife?"

"No," she said. One night he jumped as high as he could and grabbed the Blue Star. She pulled him up into the sky. She did not like being grabbed and let him go. He fell to the earth howling, as he was very scared.

Thump! He fell so fast and so hard he made a huge hole in the peak of Mount Mazama. Coyote looked around at where he was. The top of the mountain was gone and Coyote started crying. Because he had touched the Blue Star with his paw, it was now blue. He cried all night long and the next day and again the next night. He cried so long that the hole filled up with his blue tears. And that is how Crater Lake was formed. Coyote is still sad, and that is why at night you can still hear Coyote howling at the sky.

More Information

Many books share creation stories told by tribe members. Coyote and Raven are tricksters, magicians, silly, and usually get into trouble. "Three Indian Legends of the Klamaths" by Lucille Kraiman, is about how Crater Lake was formed. "Return of the Raven?" by Edison & Leatha Chiloquin is another story told in the winter months.

History of Crater Lake

John Wesley Hillman - One of the first white people (non-Indian) to see Crater Lake.

John Wesley Hillman, a prospector living in Jacksonville, along with **Isaac Skeeters** and **Henry Klippel,** were the first non-Indians to see Crater Lake, on June 12, 1853. Hillman overheard gold seekers talking about the "Lost Cabin Mine." Shortly thereafter, an item appeared in the "Rogue River Courier" a Grants Pass, Oregon, newspaper, confirming the existence of the mine, and its location in Klamath County. So Hillman, Skeeters, and Klippel set out to find the "lost" mine. Standing on what is today called "Discovery Point" on Rim Drive, Hillman saw the lake. HIllman said it was the bluest lake he had ever seen and called it "**Deep Blue Lake**." Other members of his party wanted to call the lake "**Mysterious Lake**."

Lake Majesty - Another Name for the Lake.

Fort Klamath, a military garrison, was established in 1863, to protect emigrants from the East, as well as to build roads. On August 1, 1865, **Captain Franklin B. Sprague,** of the first Oregon Volunteer Infantry, dispatched two hunters to bring back fresh meat for the crew building a road from Fort Klamath to Union Creek and the upper Rogue River. The hunters spied the lake and told Captain Sprague. Sprague assembled six men and off they went to see the lake. **Sergeant Orson Stearns** saw the lake, saw animal tracks leading down to the lake and followed them. He was the first non-Indian to climb down the caldera wall to the lake. Sprague followed Stearns down the caldera wall. Stearns exclaimed to Sprague, "This must be the sky, it is too blue to be a lake." Sprague, standing along the shoreline, called it "**Lake Majesty**."

Captain Sprague

James M. Sutton - Part of group to first explore Crater Lake by boat.

James M. Sutton was an editor of the Jacksonville newspaper. In 1869 he organized a group of men to visit the lake and explore it in a canvas boat. They reached Wizard Island and spent several hours exploring the cinder cone. When he returned to Jacksonville, Sutton wrote an article for his newspaper and called the lake "**Crater Lake**." Although the lake sits in a caldera, the name stuck. In later years he started the Ashland newspaper, The Tidings.

Captain Clarence Dutton - Maps depth of Crater Lake.

Captain Clarence Dutton, a geologist with the United States Geological Survey, in 1886 conducted a survey to map the lake, at the request of William Gladstone Steel. The report was used by Steel in his quest to make Crater Lake a National Park.

On August 1, 1886, using pipe and piano wire, Dutton took soundings (measurements of the depth of the lake) at 168 different points. His measurements showed the lake to be 1996 feet deep. Today, using sonor equipment the lake was recorded at 1932 feet (1943 is the official depth of the lake.) The difference in the water depth of the lake is due to the varying amounts of rain, snowfall, and evaporation each year. Dutton Cliff, Dutton Creek, and Dutton Creek Trail were named after Captain Clarence Dutton.

History of Crater Lake

William Gladstone Steel - Father of Crater Lake National Park.

William Gladstone Steel has been called the "Father of Crater Lake National Park." As a boy growing up in Kansas, he read about the lake in the local newspaper. He was very curious about the lake and determined to see it. Steel's family moved to Portland in 1872, when he was 18. Thirteen years later, in 1885, he made his way to the lake.

From the time he first saw the lake, he began working to have Crater Lake and the surrounding area set aside and preserved for all people for all time. On August 21, 1886, President Cleveland set aside 10 townships that included Crater Lake. Captain Dutton informed Congress in Washington, D.C. of the geological wonders of Crater Lake. On May 22, 1902, Crater Lake was established as our fifth national park and Steel's efforts over a period of 17 years were rewarded. So that he could fish in the lake, Steel introduced fish to the lake. He lowered buckets full of fish over the side of the caldera. Today kokanee salmon and rainbow trout are still in the lake. See page 51 for more information about the fish in the lake. Steel named several of the geological features of the Park, including Wizard Island, The Witches Cauldron (the crater at the top of Wizard Island), and Llao Rock.

William G. Steel named his boat "Cleetwood."

Peter Britt - Photographs Crater Lake.

Peter Britt, a resident of Jacksonville, Oregon, was the first man to photograph Crater Lake. Born in Switzerland in 1819, his family emigrated to Chicago in 1845. In 1852, he walked the Oregon Trail to Portland and then on to Jacksonville. In 1852 he opened a photo studio in Jacksonville and supplemented his income by hauling freight. He took the first picture of Crater Lake on August 13, 1874. Britt took a wet plate camera, stereo camera, darkroom tent, glass plates, various chemicals and a large container of distilled water. The journey took five days, following the Rogue River. William Steel used the photographs in his pursuit of convincing the United States Congress to establish Crater Lake National Park.

Historic Buildings

Merel S. Sager Administration Building.

The administration building, located across from the Steel Visitor Center, was built in 1934 and 1935, opening in 1936. Funding and much of the work came from the Public Works Administration (WPA) and the Civilian Conservation Corp. (CCC) helped with a few of the details. A parking lot to hold 50 cars was also built. The building was named after Merel S. Sager, the National Park Service landscape architect who designed a complex of buildings here to house National Park Service staff. In 1985 and 1986, the building was restored to its original condition and the inside adapted to modern offices.

Kiser Studio, a small stone structure west of the lodge on the Rim, was built in the summer of 1921. From the studio Fred H. Kiser led his photographic expeditions and sold his photographs. Fred H. Kiser, a photographer who grew up in the Columbia Gorge, joined William Gladstone Steel and others on a tour of Crater Lake in 1903. Fred and his brother Oscar documented the trip. They took many photographs of geological formations inside the caldera. He climbed everywhere to get a good shot of Crater Lake. From Mount Scott they took the first photographs of the entire lake. In the studio, Kiser sold photographs, post cards, and paintings. The National Park Service purchased the Kiser Studio in 1929 and has used it for a variety of interpretive purposes.

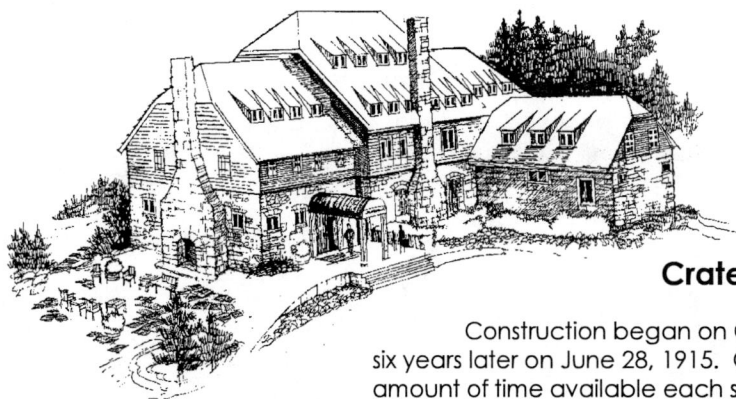

Illllustration of Crater Lake Lodge courtesy of National Park Service.

Crater Lake Lodge

Construction began on Crater Lake Lodge in 1909; the lodge opened six years later on June 28, 1915. Over 500 inches of snow a year limited the amount of time available each summer to work on the building. Stone from Garfield Peak was used on the lower story, dark brown wood above, with a steeply sloping green roof punctuated by two rows of dormer windows. Sturdy stone chimneys, made from stone quarried on Garfield Peak, tower above the lodge. The building closed in 1989 due to structural problems. After a complete reconstruction, the Lodge reopened in 1995. The Great Hall, dining room, and lobby retain the look of the original building. Today there are only 71 rooms but each has its own bathroom.

Historic Buildings

Watchman Lookout

The Watchman Lookout was built in 1931. A steep trail leads to the fire tower and museum. A wonderful spot for viewing the park. When built, the museum contained an exhibit on fire ecology. The fire tower is manned during the fire season. During the summers of 1999 and 2000, the Park Service renovated the Lookout.

Sinnott Memorial Overlook

Located on Victory Rock, the structure was completed in 1931. Oregon Congressman Nicholas J. Sinnott was an advocate not only for Crater Lake National Park, but also for all National Parks. The structure was built on Victory Rock, 50 feet below the caldera rim. Merel S. Sager was in charge of the construction of the large stone structure. Paleontologist John C. Merriam felt all National Parks should provide education programs and was instrumental, along with Congressman Sinnott, in obtaining funding for the Sinnott Memorial Overlook. In addition, Sinnott was president of the Carnegie Institution and in 1920, the institution donated $5,000 for telescopes and exhibits. A wonderful interactive exhibit in the Sinnott Memorial tells the story of the eruption of Mount Mazama. During the summer months you may see hundreds of the pandora moths resting on the walls and ceiling of the overlook.

Illustration above shows that the Sinnott Memorial Overlook was built into the caldera wall. Illustration on the right shows the parapet of the Sinnott Memorial Overlook. The view of the lake is spectacular. On the walls of the parapet are a few of the hundreds of pandora moths you may see during your visit to the park.

Red-tailed Hawk
Buteo jamaicensis

Black Bear
Ursus americana

White Sphinx Moth
Hyles lineata

Animals of Crater Lake National Park

Make Your Own Field Guide

Throughout this book you will find descriptions and drawings of plants and animals you may see at Crater Lake National Park. Some of the animals commonly seen during the day are the black-tailed deer and Douglas' squirrel. Others come out at dawn or dusk and you may not be able to see them at all, but if you look hard, you may be able to see their signs. (Each animal description includes a drawing of their tracks.)

Some of the plants you may see all year long, others only during spring and summer. Ponderosa pine keeps its leaves or needles throughout the year, while quaking aspen and other deciduous trees lose their leaves in the fall. Some of the herbaceous plants are perenials and the tops die out in the fall, but sprout in the spring.

Instructions: Read the information about the plants and animals that live in or visit Crater Lake National Park. After you have read the information, answer the question at the bottom and then cut it out to make a field guide.

American Kestrel, *Falco sparverius*
Formerly called the sparrow hawk. A small falcon, bright rusty back and tail and blue-gray wings. Cheeks are white with two vertical black stripes. Female larger than male. **Length**: 8 - 15". **Wingspan**: 20 - 24". **Weight**: 3.4 - 5.3 oz. **Habitat**: Often seen perching on telephone wires. Open country, urban areas, trees. **Call**: *klee-klee-klee-klee*. **Diet**: Insects, small mammals and birds, reptiles. **Nest**: Little nesting material in tree or cliff cavity. **Eggs**: 3 - 7 whitish/pinkish, marked with brown or lavender.

Where might you see me as you drive along park roads?

_____

Illustration of a sample field guide page.

Throughout this book are field guide pages of plants and animals. They are placed so you may make your own nature field guide. Cut out each description section. Glue them to a piece of constuction paper or laminate each plant or animal, punch a hole in the top and bottom left corners, tie them together with a piece of string, yarn, or ribbon, and you will have a small, compact field guide to take with you whenever you visit Crater Lake National Park, or other parks in our area.

Red Columbine, *Aquilegia formosa*
Member of the buttercup family. Also called the crimson columbine and the Sitka columbine.
Plant: 6 - 26" high. A bushy plant with several stems and many divided leaves. **Leaves**: Divided into leaflets 3/4 - 1½" long, each lobed and cleft across ends.
Flowers: 2" wide, handsome red and yellow flowers hang at the end of branches.
Pollinator: Hummingbirds.
Blooms: July and August.
Habitat: Open woods, on banks, near seeps. **Location in Park**: May be seen at numerous places in the rocky cliffs around the rim, at Vidae Falls, and in the Castle Crest Wildflower Garden. **Tidbit**: The species name *formosa*, Latin for beautiful, aptly describes this plant.

What animal pollinates the red columbine?

American Marten, *Martes americana*
Diurnal (active during daylight. Also called Pine Marten, "American Sable." Member of the weasel family. A long, low-slung body, short legs, short rounded ears, and a thick silky coat. Brownish, with paler head and underparts, orange or buff throat patch. **Breeding**: Mate midsummer. Two to four young born blind, nest in hollow logs and trees, usually in April. **Habitat**: Forests, particularly coniferous. Dens in fallen logs or tree holes. **Diet**: Squirrels, rabbits, mice, and birds; also carrion, eggs, berries, conifer seeds, and honey. **Tidbit**: They have one litter of two to six newborn a year.

Where will you find my den?

Mammals Seldom Seen in the Park

As you walk around the park you may see a black-tailed deer wandering through the park or a golden-mantled ground squirrel scampering around whitebark pine trees. Over 50 different species of mammals may be seen in the park if you are there at just the right time.

Instructions: In the list below are some of the many animals that live in the park but are rarely seen. Illustrated below are some of the mammals and their tracks. Place the number of the mammal on the line below the mammal and its track. If you see one of the mammal tracks on the trail, circle the name of the mammal. **Hint**: If you do not know the name of the animal, the scientific name will help you find the common name on the *Mammals Checklist*.

1 - American Badger
2 - American Beaver
3 - Fisher

4 - Muskrat
5 - Pronghorn Antelope

6 - Snowshoe Hare
7 - Spotted Skunk
8 - Virginia Opossum

Lepus americanus

Color me brown with a white tail in the summer and white in the winter, sometimes with brown spots.

Spilogale pitorius

Color me black with white spots.

Ondatra zibethica

Color me dark brown above and paler on sides with nearly white on throat

Didelphis marsupalis

Color me white with gray and black-tipped hairs, with black ears with pink tips and black patches around the eyes.

Taxidea taxus

Color me yellowish-gray with white stripe from snout to shoulder.

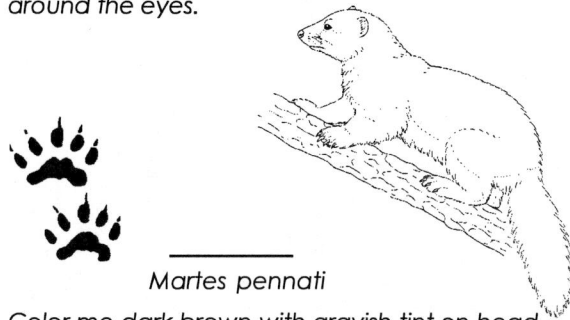

Martes pennati

Color me dark brown with grayish tint on head.

Castor canadensis

Color me dark brown with black tail and black feet.

Antilocapro americana

Color my upper body and outside legs pale tan or reddish-brown, black patches on face and neck.

Mammals of Crater Lake National Park
Crossword Puzzle

On the line provided next to each mamal write in the date you saw it or its track.   Record more observations on the journal pages at the back of the book. Observations can include: location of the mammal, coloration, track prints, weather conditions, or draw a picture of the animal or track.

Summer/Winter: A - Abundant, C - Common, U - Uncommon, P - Present, but not often seen. R - Rare, -- Not seen in winter

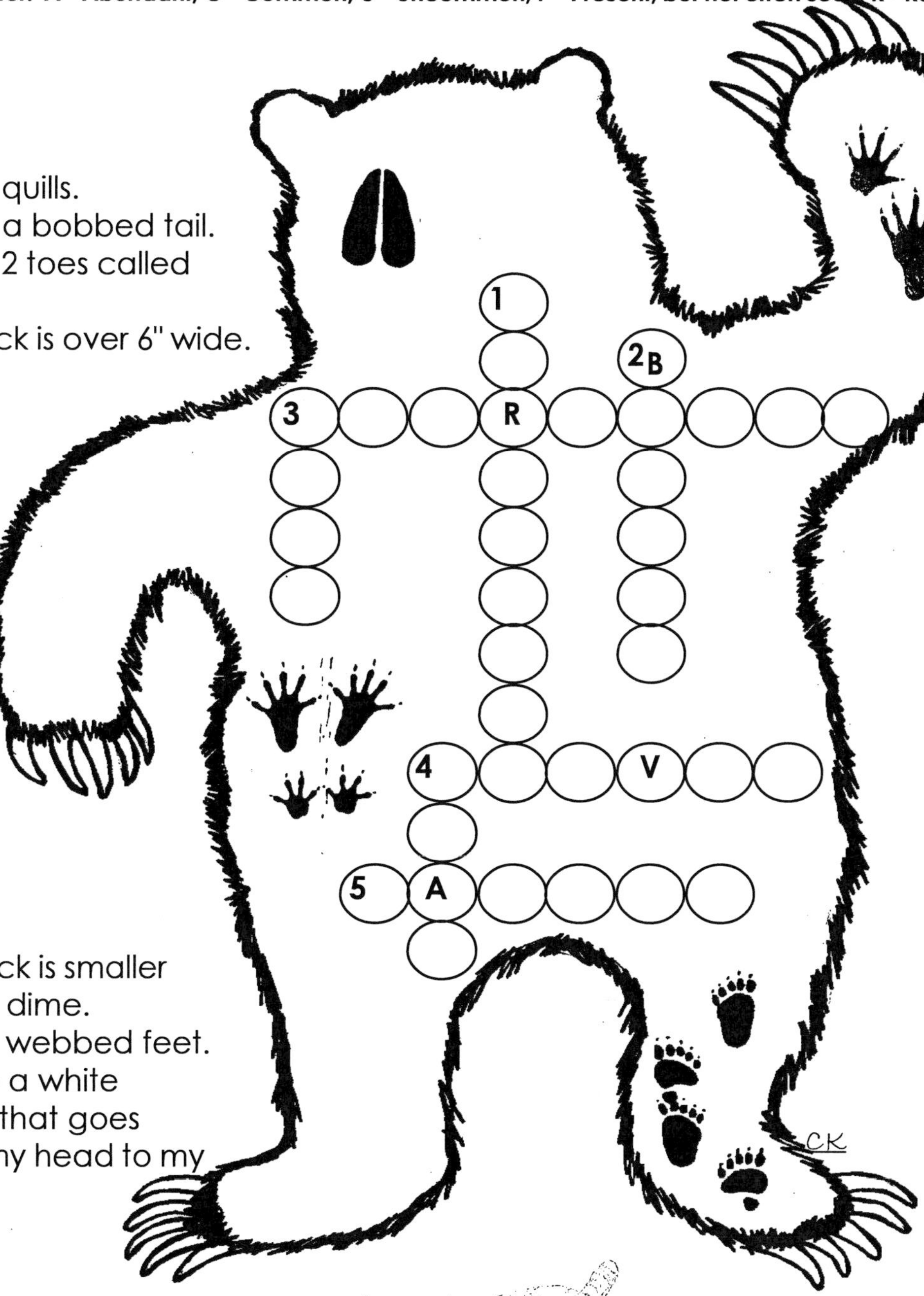

Down
1 - I have quills.
2 - I have a bobbed tail.
3 - I have 2 toes called hoofs.
4 - My track is over 6" wide.

Across
3 - My track is smaller than a dime.
4 - I have webbed feet.
5 - I have a white stripe that goes from my head to my tail.

Porcupine
Erethizon dorsatum

Bobcat
Lynx rufus

American Badger
Taxidea taxus

-35-

Checklist - Mammals at Crater Lake National Park

On the line provided next to each mamal write in the date you saw it or its track.   Record more observations on the journal pages at the back of the book. Observations can include: location of the mammal, coloration, track prints, weather conditions, or draw a picture of the animal or track.
Summer/Winter: A - Abundant, C - Common, U - Uncommon, P - Present, but not often seen, R - Rare, -- Not seen in winter

_____**American Badger** *Taxidea taxus* - C/P	
_____**American Beaver** *Castor canadensis* - R/R	
_____**American Marten** (Pine Marten) *Martes americana* - C/C	
_____**American Pika** *Ochotona princeps* - C/P	
_____**American Shrew Mole** *Neurotrichus gibbsii* - C/P	
_____**Belding's Ground Squirrel** *Spermophilus beldingi*- R/R	
_____**Big Brown Bat** *Eptesicus fuscus* - C/--	
_____**Black Bear** *Ursus americanus* - C/P	
_____**Bobcat** *Lynx rufus* - R/R	
_____**Botta Pocket Gopher** *Thomomys bottae* - U/P	
_____**Bushy-tailed Woodrat** *Neotoma cinerea* - C/P	
_____**California Ground Squirrel** *Spermophilus beecheyi* - C/P	
_____**Cascade Red Fox** *Vulpes vulpes* - C/R	
_____**Coyote** *Canis latrans* - C/C	
_____**Creeping Vole (Oregon Vole)** *Microtus oregoni* - U/P	
_____**Deer Mouse** *Peromyscus maniculatus* - A/P	
_____**Douglas' Squirrel** *Tamiasciurus douglasii* - A/P	
_____**Dusky-footed Woodrat** *Neotoma fuscipes* - U/P	
_____**Fisher** *Martes pennanti* - R/P	
_____**Golden-mantled Ground Squirrel**	
Spermophiluis lateralis - A/P	
_____**Gray Fox** *Urocyon cinereoargenteus* - U/R	
_____**Hoary Bat** *Lasiurus cinereus* - C/--	
_____**Little Brown Myotis** *Myotis lucifugus* - C/--	
_____**Long-tailed Vole** *Microtus longicaudus* - C/P	
_____**Long-tailed Weasel** *Mustela frenata* - C/P	
_____**Mink** *Mustela vison* - R/R	
_____**Mountain Lion (Cougar, Puma)** *Felis concolor* - R/R	
_____**Mule or Black-tailed Deer** *Odocoileus hemionus* - C/R	
_____**Muskrat** *Ondatra zibethica* - R/R	
_____**Northern Flying Squirrel** *Glaucomys sabrinus*- C/P	
_____**Porcupine** *Erethizon dorsatum* - C/P	
_____**Pronghorn** *Antilocapra americana* - R/R	
_____**Raccoon** *Procyon lotor* - R/P	
_____**Rocky Mountain Elk** *Cervus canadensis nelsonii* - C/R	
_____**Snowshoe Hare** *Lepus americanus*- C /U	
_____**Spotted Skunk** *Spilogale putorius* - U/R	
_____**Striped Skunk** *Mephitis mephitis* - C/R	
_____**Townsend's Chipmunk** *Tamias townsendii* - A/P	
_____**Townsend's Vole** *Microtus townsendii* - C/P	
_____**Vagrant Shrew** *Sorex vagrans* - C/P	
_____**Virginia Opossum** *Didelphis marsupialis* - U/P	
_____**Water Shrew** *Sorex palustris* - C/P	
_____**Western Gray Squirrel** *Sciurus griseus* - U/U	
_____**Western Jumping Mouse** *Zapus princeps* - C/P	
_____**Western Pocket Gopher** *Thomomys mazama* - C/P	
_____**White-tailed Jackrabbit** *Lepus townsendii* - U/U	
_____**Wolverine** *Gulo gulo* - R/R	
_____**Yellow Pine Chipmunk** *Tamias amoenus* - C/P	
_____**Yellow-bellied Marmot** *Marmota flaviventris* - C/P	
_____**Yuma Myotis** *Myotis yumanensis* - R/R	

Key to Mammal Tracks

Most of the mammals living in or visiting Crater Lake National Park are active late at night or very early in the morning. To find out which animals have been here, you can look for their tracks. This key will help you. **Instructions:** A key is a way to figure out what you are looking at by process of elimination. Keys are used to identify plants, rocks, and even animal tracks. With any key, you are given two options. Select the option that best fits the tracks you see. Then go to the next set of options, until you have identified the tracks. Have fun learning to key-out the animal tracks.

Front   **Rear**

1a Tracks with two toes (hooves)	Go to 2	
1b Tracks with four or five toes	Go to 3	
2a Hooves are less than 4 inches long	Mule Deer	
2b Hooves are more than 4 inches long	Elk (Cattle)	
3a Four toes front and back	Go to 4	
3b Four toes in front, five back or Five toes front and back	Go to 5	
4a Toe nails present	Coyote	
4b Toe nails absent	Snowshoe Hare	
5a Toes five front and back	Black Bear	
5b Toes four in front, five back	Go to 6	
6a Tracks more than 3 inches long	Porcupine	
6b Tracks 2.5 inches long or less	Go to 7	
7a Tracks about 1.5 inches long or less	American Marten	
7b Tracks about 2 inches long	Yellow-bellied Marmot	

Some Mammals of Crater Lake National Park

Black Bear, *Ursus americanus*
Nocturnal. **Length:** 4 to 6 feet. **Weight:** 50 to 200 pounds. Black, cinnamon or blue gray with a white patch on its chest. Its face is brown and roundish, with small eyes and small, round, erect ears. They have strong claws used for digging, tearing, and climbing. **Habitat:** Primarily mountain areas. Dens where the bears overwinter are usually in a cave, hollow log or strump, or the base of a hollow tree. May be seen anywhere in the park as they roam large distances. **Diet:** Primarily vegetarian but will eat fish, insects, mammals, and refuse. **Tidbit:** Their eyesight is poor, but they have an excellent sense of smell. They can run up to 30 miles per hour, and are good swimmers.

How do bears spend their winters?

_____

Northern Flying Squirrel *Glaucomys sabrinus*
Nocturnal. **Length:** 10 - 15". Very soft brown fur above, white below. A loose fold of skin between fore and hind legs. Large black eyes. **Habitat:** Coniferous forests, mixed forests, and sometimes in hardwoods where old or dead trees have numerous woodpecker-type nesting holes, especially in stumps. May be seen in lower elevation old growth Douglas-fir forests on the west side of the park. **Diet:** Nuts and seeds but also eats insects. Stores food for winter use. **Nest:** Shredded bark in tree hollows or abandoned bird's nest. **Litter:** 2 - 5 young are born in spring. **Tidbit:** It spreads its legs and stretches its flight skin as it glids from tree to tree, pulling upright at the last instant to land gently.

Why do flying squirrels fly?

_____

Porcupine, *Erethizon dorsatum*
Nocturnal, but suns in trees. Brown to yellowish brown in color, chunky mammal with high arching back and long coat of sharp, barbed quills. **Length** - 25 ½ to 40". **Weight:** 7 3/4 to 40 lbs. **Tracks:** Hind foot 3 to 4" long. 5 toes on hind foot. Pebbled knobs on feet leave stippled mark. **Habitat:** Lodgepole pine forests in the park. **Sign:** Twigs with bark chewed off, found at base of trees. **Diet:** Herbivore. Feeds on leaves, twigs, and such green plants as skunk cabbage, lupines, and clover. They especially like wild roses. In winter it chews through the bark to get at the inner bark (cambium). Fond of salt. **Breeding:** Mates in fall. One young born in May or June, headfirst with soft quills aimed backwards. Quills harden within half an hour. **Tidbit:** Often seen as a black ball perching high in a tree and may perch in a tree for days, chewing the bark. When alarmed, flips tail, releasing quills from skin. Quills are not thrown.

How many young do I give birth to?

_____

Golden-mantled Ground Squirrel, *Spermophilus lateralis*
Chipmunk-like. Back gray, brownish, or buff; belly whitish. Head and shoulders coppery red, forming "golden mantle." On sides 1 white strip bordered by black stripes; no facial stripes. **Length** - 9 to 12". **Weight** - 6 - 9 ½ ounces. **Tracks:** Hind track about an inch long and has 5 toes. **Habitat:** Lives in high mountain evergreen forests and above timberline. It usually digs its burrow among the rocks or underground, up to 100' long. Opening to burrow often under logs, tree roots, or boulders. **Diet:** Seeds, nuts, fruits as well as green vegetation and insects. **Breeding:** One litter per year with 4 to 6 young born in summer. **Winter:** Prepares for winter by adding layers of fat. When snow covers the ground, it curls up in its snug burrow to sleep all winter, usually October to May.

Where do I live?

_____

Some Mammals of Crater Lake National Park

Deer Mouse, *Peromyscus maniculatus*
This small field mouse weighs up to 0.5 ounces, has a long, hairy tail, big ears, and eyes. Foot track is smaller than a dime. Adults are reddish brown on back with white belly. Juveniles are dark gray on the back with a pale grey belly. **Habitat:** Lives in burrows in riparian woodlands, fields, grasslands, and forests. May be found everywhere in the park. **Diet:** Seeds, nuts, fruits, berries, and insects. Leaves a cache of seeds in protected areas for later use.

What is the size of my footprint?

_____

Bushy-tailed Woodrat, *Neotoma cinerea*
Nocturnal. Tan above peppered with black above, white below. Bushy, squirrel-like tail. **Length** - 11 to 18 ½". **Weight:** 5½ to 15½ ounces. **Habitat:** coniferous forests and rocky areas. In coniferous forests may build its home as high as 50' up a tree. May be seen in old growth forests on westside of park. **Diet:** Green vegetation, twigs, nuts, seeds, mushrooms, and some animal matter. **Breeding:** 1 - 2 litters a year with 2 - 6 young, born May through September. **Sign:** Large nest of sticks under log, in crevices, or in abandoned buildings. **Tidbit:** Also called "packrat or trade rat" because it stashes anything shiny that catches its eye. If he is already carrying something he may drop it for the new treasure, which makes people say that he is "trading." The bushy tail is used for balance when climbing or jumping.

What is my other name?

_____

Long-tailed Weasel, *Mustela frenata*
Nocturnal. Carnivore. Short legs and a black nose, black eyes, and a black-tipped tail. Light yellow and tan coat. Coat may turn white in winter. **Length:** 11 to 21". **Tracks:** Hind print about 1" wide and often only show 4 of the 5 toes. **Habitat:** Forests, brushy, and open areas; prefers to be near or along streams. **Diet:** Mice and other rodents, snakes, birds. **Breeding:** Mates midsummer. 3 - 9 young born blind, nearly naked in early May. **Tidbit:** Hides caches of dead mice under logs or in burrow.

What color am I?

_____

Beaver, *Castor canadensis*
Largest rodent in North America. 2 1/2' to 4' in length, weighs 30 to 60 pounds. Has large, webbed hind feet and a paddle-shaped hairless tail. Fur coat is dense and soft, short underfur and coarse, shiny overhairs reddish brown to dark brown to black, with a lighter belly. Feet and tail black. **Habitat:** Rivers, streams, ponds, and lakes. May be seen in streams near the parks boundary. **Breeding:** January through March; single litter per year with three to four young. **Diet:** Bark of red alder, cottonwood, willow, Douglas-fir, western hemlock, and quaking aspen, salmonberry, salal, deer fern, swordfern, sedges, skunk cabbage. **Tidbits:** Mainly nocturnal.

Which trees do I like to eat?

_____

Birds of Crater Lake Word Search

Instructions: Part I - Listed below are names of more birds you may see on your visit to Crater Lake National Park. Words in **bold** may be found backwards, forward, up, down, or diagonally. Circle the letters of the words. Write the uncircled letters on the line below. The uncircled letters spell the names of two more birds you may see in the Park.

_____

Barred Owl
Black-backed Woodpecker
California **Gull**
Common **Nighthawk**
Common **Raven**
Cooper's Hawk
Dark-**eyed** Junco
Horned **Lark**

Lincoln's Sparrow
Mallard
Northern **Goshawk**
Northern **Pygmy** Owl

Northern **Saw-whet** Owl
Red-breasted Nuthatch
Red **Crossbill**
Swainson's **Thrush**
White-crowned Sparrow
Vaux's Swift
Yellow-rumped Warbler

Northern Saw-whet Owl
Aegolius acadicus

Black-backed Wood pecker
Picoides arcticus

Northern Goshawk
Accipter gentilis

Barred Owl
Strix varia

White-crowned Sparrow
Zonotricyia leucophrys

Red Crossbill
Loxia curvirostra

```
Y B L A C K B A C K E D P
D E R C A I V R N I E G E
R ☺ L K O A F I A N U G R
A A R L U O G L W L L O E
L A V X O H P O L L C S D
L W S E T W R E I O N H B
A S O H N C R B R L E A R
M A A D E N S U O S Y W E
& W G T E S Y C M O E K A
K W I L O R N M D P D E S
N H C R R I R O G W E N T
W E C E L D K A I Y˛N D E
G T H R U S H L B E P T D
```

CK

-40-

Checklist - Birds at Crater Lake National Park

On the line provided next to the bird's name, write in the date you saw it. You can record additional observations about the birds on the journal pages at the back of the book.

*Seen Year round
**Nests in Park

_____ **American Dipper*** *Cinclus mexicanus*
_____ **American Robin*** *Turdus migratorius*
_____ **Belted Kingfisher** *Ceryle alcyon*
_____ **Black-backed Woodpecker** *Picoides arcticus*
_____ **Brown Creeper*** *Certhia americana*
_____ **California Gull** *Larus californicus*
_____ **Cassin's Finch** *Carpodacus cassinii*
_____ **Chipping Sparrow**** *Spizella passerina*
_____ **Clark's Nutcracker*** *Nucifraga columbia*
_____ **Common Merganser** *Mergus merganser*
_____ **Common Nighthawk*** *Chordeiles minor*
_____ **Common Raven** *Corvus corax*
_____ **Dark-eyed Junco*** *Junco hyemalis*
_____ **Double-crested Cormorant** *Phalacrocorax auritus*
_____ **Evening Grosbeak*** *Hesperiphona vespertina*
_____ **Golden-crowned Kinglet*** *Regulus satrapa*
_____ **Gray Jay*** *Perisoreus canadensis*
_____ **Gray-crowned Rosy Finch** *Leucosticte tephrocotis*
_____ **Great Blue Heron** *Ardea herodias*
_____ **Hairy Woodpecker*** *Picoides villosus*
_____ **Hermit Thrush *** *Catharus guttatus*
_____ **Horned Lark**** *Eremophila alpestris*
_____ **Killdeer** *Charadrius vociferus*
_____ **Lincoln's Sparrow**** *Melospiza loincolnii*
_____ **Mallard** *Anas platyrhynchos*
_____ **Mountain Bluebird** *Sialia currucoides*
_____ **Mountain Chickadee*** *Parus gambeli*
_____ **Northern Flicker*** *Colaptes auratus*
_____ **Olive-sided Flycatcher**** *Contopus borealis*
_____ **Pacific Slope Flycatcher** *Empidonax difficilis*
_____ **Pileated Woodpecker**** *Dryocopos pileatus*
_____ **Pine Siskin**** *Carduelis pinus*
_____ **Red-breasted Nuthatch*** *Sitta canadensis*
_____ **Red-breasted Sapsucker** *Sphyrapicus ruber*
_____ **Red Crossbill*** *Loxia curvirostra*
_____ **Rock Wren** *Salpinctes obsoletus*
_____ **Ruffed Grouse**** *Bonasa umbellus*
_____ **Rufous Hummingbird**** *Selasporus rufus*
_____ **Sooty Grouse*** *Dendragapus fuliginosis*
_____ **Spotted Sandpiper**** *Actitis solitaria*
_____ **Steller's Jay**** *Cyanocitta stelleri*
_____ **Swainson's Thrush** *Catharus ustulatus*
_____ **Towsend's Solitaire**** *Myadestes townsendi*
_____ **Varied Thrush** *Ixoreus naevius*
_____ **Vaux's Swift** *Chaetura vauxi*
_____ **Warbling Vireo**** *Vireo gilvus*
_____ **Western Bluebird** *Sialia mexicana*
_____ **Western Tanager** *Piranga ludoviciana*
_____ **White-crowned Sparrow**** *Zonotrichia leucophrys*
_____ **Wilson's Warbler** *Wilsonia pusilla*
_____ **Winter Wren*** *Troglodytes troglodytes*
_____ **Yellow-rumped Warbler** *Dendroica cornata*

Birds of Crater Lake Puzzle

Instructions: Illustrated below are some of the birds you may see at Crater Lake National Park. Words in **bold** can be found in the puzzle below. The first letter of several of the words has been provided to start you out.

Gray Jay
Perisoreus canadensis
Dove gray above, paler gray below, white on head, face, and neck. Commonly seen in park **year** round.

Spotted **Sandpiper**
Actitis macularia
Brown above, white below, evenly spotted with black. **Commonly** seen in park in summer and fall.

Western **Tanager**
Piranga ludoviciana
Male head is red, back is black, below is yellow. Female is brownish above and dull **yellow** below. Commonly seen in park in summer and rarely seen in spring and fall.

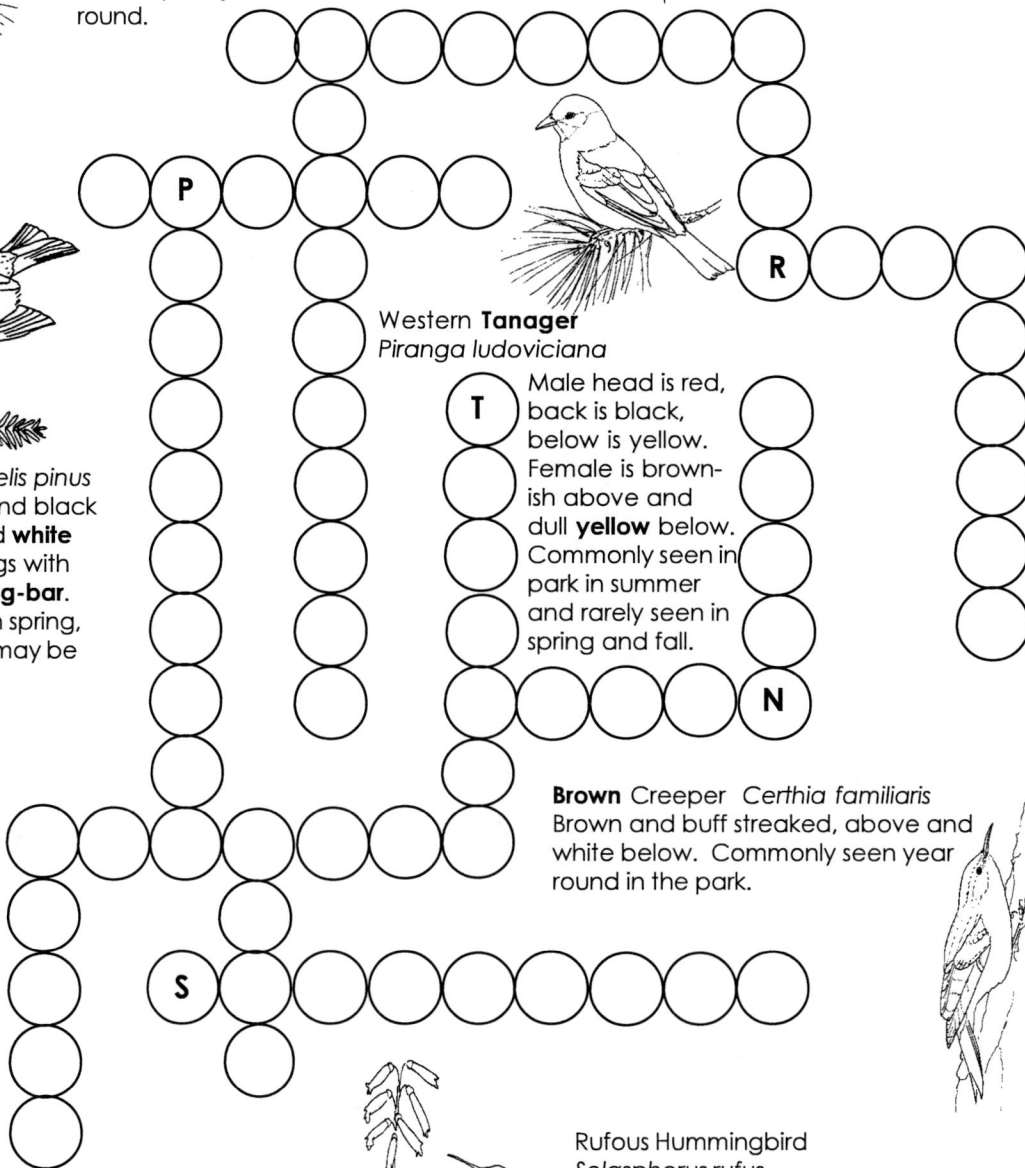

Pine Siskin *Carduelis pinus*
Streaked brown and black above, brown and **white** below. Black wings with double yellow **wing-bar**. Commonly seen in spring, summer, fall, and may be seen in winter.

Brown Creeper *Certhia familiaris*
Brown and buff streaked, above and white below. Commonly seen year round in the park.

Olive-sided Flycatcher *Contopus borealis*
Olive-brown upper body with white tufts. Heavily streaked breast and white throat. Commonly seen in park in **spring** and summer.

Rufous Hummingbird
Selasphorus rufus
Male: Reddish on body with **green** wings and ruby-colored throat. Female: green above, ruby below with **ruby** spots on throat. Commonly seen in summer in park.

Birds of Crater Lake

Crater Lake National Park provides habitat for birds that offer food, shelter, water, and protection from predators. Each of these habitats are found at varying altitudes in the park - from 4,400' to 8,926'. Birds live in or visit different areas of the park, depending upon their adaptations. Habitats include forests, wetlands, desert, and subalpine (near and above the point where few plants grow).

Instructions: Illustrated below are some of the birds you may see while visiting the park. Below each bird is information about its diet. That may help you to identify which habitat each bird visits or lives in. Place the number of the habitat in the box next to each of the birds.

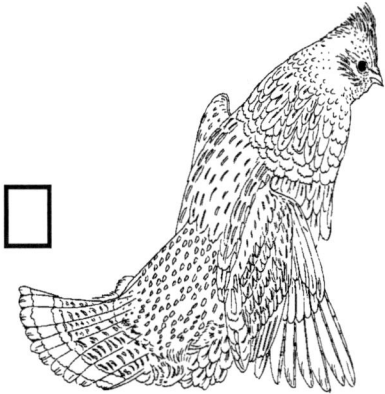

Ruffed Grouse
Diet: 80% buds, leaves, flowers, seeds and fruit; 20% insects, spiders, snails.

American Dipper/Water Ouzel
Diet: Fish, aquatic insects, aquatic plants.

Bald Eagle
Diet: Fish, usually hovers 30' - 100' and dives when one is spotted.

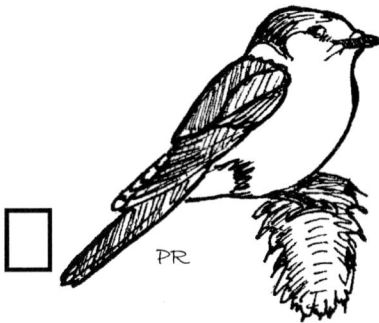

Gray Jay
Diet: Insects, fruit.

1 - Forest

2 - Streams & Creeks

3 - Lake

Cormorant
Diet: Fish, rarely aquatic insects

Spotted Sandpiper
Diet: Fish, aquatic insects, aquatic plants.

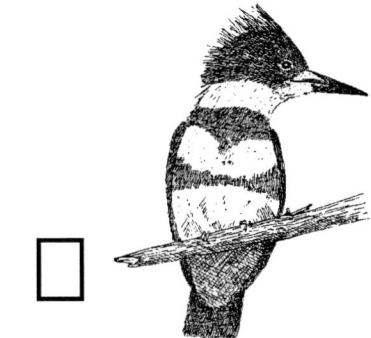

Belted Kingfisher
Diet: Fish, occasionally aquatic insects, amphibians.

Sooty Grouse
Diet: Pine cone seeds, also flowers, grasshoppers.

-43-

Clark's Nutcracker and the Whitebark Pine Tree

Clark's Nutcracker, *Nucifraga columbiana*

A member of the jay family. A dove-gray bird with long black wings, short black central tail feathers, and a long black, spike-like bill. White wing patches and white outer tail feathers are conspicuous in flight. Wingbeats are deep, slow, crowlike. **Length:** 11 - 12". **Wingspan:** 24". **Weight:** 4.6 oz. **Habitat:** High coniferous forests at timberline. **Calls:** *Shraaaaaaa, taaar,* and a hoarse, scraping *kra-a-a-a-a,* audible at some distance. **Diet:** Whitebark pine nuts, also other seeds, fruit, insects, small vertebrates, bird eggs and nestlings. Nutcracker's need approximately 20,000 pine seeds to live through the winter, an additional 5,000 seeds are needed for each chick.
Breeding Displays: Long courtship flights of male following female.
Nest: On horizontal limb, platform of twigs secured with bark strips support inner cup of fine bark strips, grass, conifer needles, feathers.
Eggs: 2 - 6 pale green, marked with brown, olive, or gray. **Tidbit:** The survival of the whitebark pine is closely related to the Clark's nutcracker. The nutcracker sometimes overlooks the caches where it stores its seeds. Those caches may become stands of new trees - a whitebark Pine forest. Caches often hold 5 - 15 conifer seeds each. They must recover at least 1,000 caches to survive the harsh winters.

Sublingual pouch (the opening to the pouch lies under the tongue) enables the nutcracker to transport up to 95 pine seeds per trip.

Using its long, pointed black bill, the nutcracker pries and pulls the seeds from the cone.

The nutcracker burying its seeds in one of many caches around the park.

Clark's Nutcracker and the Whitebark Pine Tree
Crossword Puzzle

Instructions: Answer the questions below and fill in the blanks in the crossword puzzle. Use the letter hints in the puzzle to help you. All of the answers are underlined and are on the previous page - Clark's Nutcracker and the Whitebark Pine Tree.

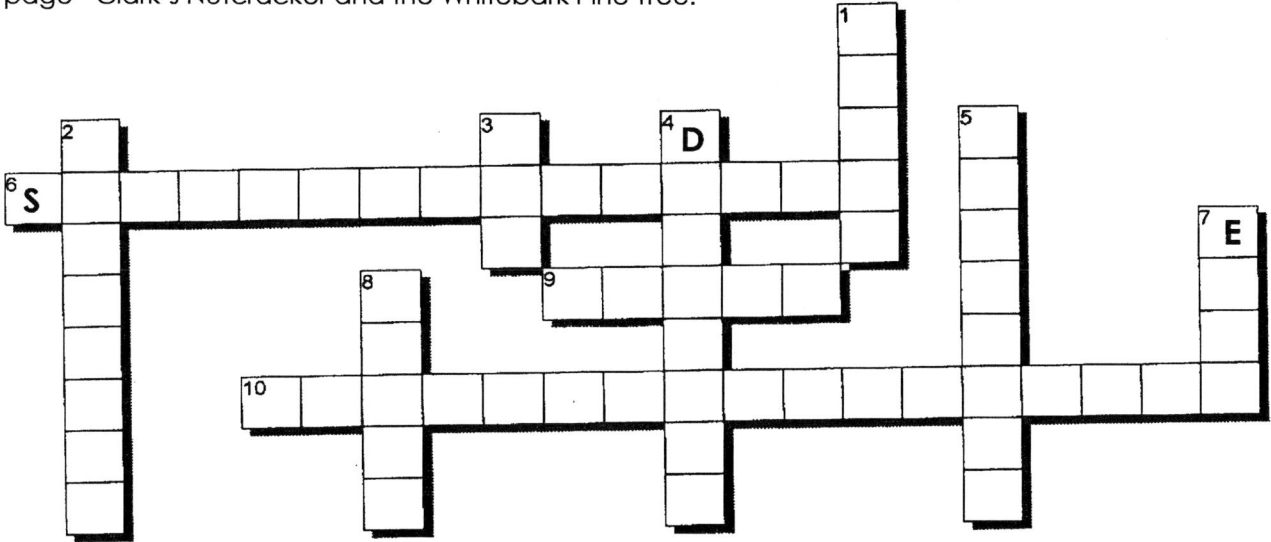

ACROSS

6) This is where I carry my seeds.
9) I need more than 20,000 to survive the winter.
10) My diet consists of small vertebrates and _____.

DOWN

1) Where I store my seeds.
2) The whitebark pine depends upon me for its _____.
3) I am a member of this family.
4) What color am I?
5) What happens to seeds I do not find?
7) I lay between 2 and 6 pale green ____.
8) What is my nest made of?

Clark's nutcracker nest with 2 pale green eggs marked with brown spots.

Clark's nutcracker twig nest with 2 chicks.

Checklist of Raptors (Birds of Prey)

On the line provided next to the bird's name, write in the date you saw it. You can record additional observations about the birds on the journal pages at the back of the book.

*Seen Year round
**Nests in the Park

_____	**American Kestrel**** *Falco sparverius*
_____	**Bald Eagle** *Haliaeetus leucocephalus*
_____	**Barred Owl** *Strix varia*
_____	**Coopers Hawk** *Accipter cooperii*
_____	**Golden Eagle** *Aquila chrysaetos*
_____	**Great Gray Owl*** *Strix nebulosa*
_____	**Great Horned Owl*** *Bubo virginianus*
_____	**Long-eared Owl** *Aslo otus*
_____	**Northern Goshawk** *Accipter gentilis*
_____	**Northern Pygmy Owl** *Glaucidium gnoma*
_____	**Northern Saw-whet Owl** *Aegolius acadicus*
_____	**Osprey** *Pandon haliaetus*
_____	**Peregrine Falcon** *Falco peregrinus*
_____	**Prairie Falcon** *Falco mexicanus*
_____	**Red-tailed Hawk*** *Buteo jamaicensis*
_____	**Sharp-shinned Hawk** *Accipiter striatus*
_____	**Spotted Owl*** *Strix occidentalis*
_____	**Turkey Vulture** *Cathartes aura*
_____	**Western Screech Owl** *Otus kennicottii*

Owl Tracks

Osprey
Pandon haliaetus

Eagle Tracks

Great Gray Owl
Strix nebulosa

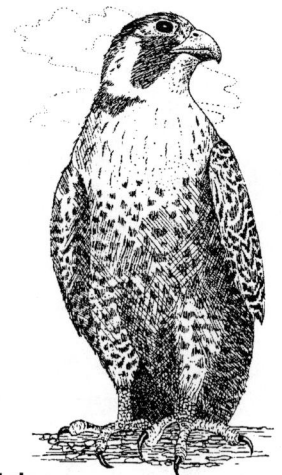

Peregrine Falco
Falco peregrinus

Birds of Prey - Hawks, Falcons, Owls, & Vultures

American Kestrel, *Falco sparverius*
Formerly called the sparrow hawk. A small falcon, bright rusty back and tail and blue-gray wings, female has rusty wings. Cheeks are white with two vertical black stripes. Female larger than male.
Length: 8 - 15". **Wingspan:** 20 - 24". **Weight:** 3.4 - 5.3 oz.
Habitat: Open country, urban areas, forests. **Call:** *klee-klee-klee-klee.* **Diet:** Insects, small mammals and birds, reptiles.
Breeding Trait: Male flies rapidly in wide circles above perch, courtship feeding, calls, pair bow, female constantly calling. **Nest:** Little nesting material in tree or cliff cavity. **Eggs:** 3 - 7 whitish/pinkish, marked with brown or lavender. **Spotted in Park:** Whitebark pine forests, mountain hemlock forest, ponderosa pine forest.

How many eggs do I lay?

_____

Red-tailed Hawk, *Buteo jamaicensis*
Reddish colored uppertail, paler red undertail, white chest with contrasting dark streaks, hooked bill, and sharp talons. Wings are broad and fairly rounded. Keen eyesight. Rides the thermals -- warm air currents -- soaring in a circle pattern of flight to conserve energy. Most common species of hawk. Farmers like them because they keep rodent populations under control.
Length: 17 - 22". **Wingspan:** 47 - 56". **Weight:** 1.5 - 3.3 lbs.
Call: A loud, harsh scream - *keeeyerr, keeeyerr.*
Diet: Rodents, birds, reptiles, fish, insects. **Breeding Traits:** Aerial display, male stoop at female, courtship feeding.
Nests: Bulky stick and twig nest lined with bark in tree tops or high on cliffs. **Eggs:** 1 - 5 white/bluish-white, spotted with brown or unmarked. **Spotted in Park:** Whitebark pine forests, ponderosa pine forest,

What is my nest made of?

_____

Great Horned Owl *Bubo virginianus*
A large owl with ear tufts or horns. Conspicuous white throat bib with heavy bars beneath. Fluffy plumage makes flight almost soundless. In flight it looks neckless, large-headed.
Length: 18 - 25". **Weight:** 3.1 lbs. **Habitat:** Forests, woodlots, streamsides, open country. **Call:** Hoo! Hu-hu-hu, Hoo! Hoo! **Diet:** Rabbits and rodents, birds, fish, amphibians, reptiles, insects.
Breeding Traits: Aerial displays, calls, courtship feeding. **Nest:** In tree cavity, cave, crevice, or stump filled with moss, sticks, hair, shredded bark. **Eggs:** 1 - 4, dull white. **Spotted in Park:** Mountain hemlock forest, ponderosa pine forest.

Name 2 ways I attract a female (breeding).

_____

Turkey Vulture, *Cathartes aura*
A large, eagle-like bird. brown-black with a featherless red head, ivory beak, and yellow feet. Distinctive "V" wing flying pattern as it soars over open meadows and grasslands searching for carrion. **Length:** 24 - 32". **Wingspan:** 63 - 72". **Weight:** 3.5 - 5.3 lbs.
Habitat: Open country, grasslands, forests
Call: A silent bird, but will hiss or groan occasionally. **Diet:** Consumes any dead animal. **Breeding Traits:** Males dive at female, female follows male in flight. **Nest:** No nest. Lays eggs on snags, in caves, or hollow stump. **Eggs:** 1 - 3, white occasionally marked with brown spots.

Name 2 places where I lay my eggs?

_____

Amphibians & Reptiles

Instructions: On the line provided next to each animal write in the date you saw it or its track. In your journal you can record more observations: location of the amphibian or reptile, coloration, track prints, weather conditions or draw a picture of the animal or its track.

Amphibian

_____**Cascades Frog** *Rana cascadae*
_____**Long-toed Salamander** *Ambystoma macrodactylum*
_____**Pacific Giant Salamander** *Dicamptodon eschscholtzii*
_____**Pacific Tree Frog** *Pseudacris (Hyla) regilla*
_____**Rough-skinned Newt** *Taricha granulosa*
_____**Tailed Frog** *Ascaphus truei*
_____**Western Toad** *Bufo boreas*

Reptile

_____**Common Garter Snake** *Thamnophis sirtalis*
_____**Northern Alligator Lizard** *Elgaria coerulea*
_____**Northern Sagebrush Lizard** *Sceloporus graciosus*
_____**Northwestern Garter Snake** *Thamnophis ordinoides*
_____**Racer** *Coluber constrictor*
_____**Rubber Boa** *Charina bottae*
_____**Short-horned Lizard** *Phrynosoma douglassii*
_____**Western Skink** *Eumeces skiltonianus*
_____**Western Terrestrial Garter Snake** *Thamnophis elegans*

Lateral Undulating Snake Trail

Snake Trail

Shed Snake Skin

Frog Tracks

Garter Snake found at various locations around the park.

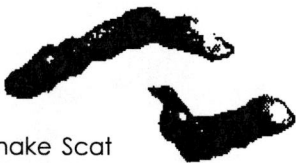

Snake Scat
4 x 0.4 in
10 x 1 cm

The Garter Snake adapted to living on Wizard Island. Without the stripes it blends in with the pumice rock and may be safer from hawks and other predators.

Amphibians

Although winters are long and harsh at Crater Lake, amphibians and reptiles do live in the park. As with other animals who spend the winter at Crater Lake, they have adapted to their environment. Some of the amphibians and reptiles who live at Crater Lake are listed in the checklist on page 48.

Amphibians spend part of their lives in water and part on land. Amphibians include frogs, toads, salamanders, and newts. They have moist skin and live in cool, damp places to protect themselves from drying out. Most amphibians lay their eggs in water. Like reptiles, amphibians are cold-blooded - their body temperature stays about the same as the temperature of their surroundings. To stay alive these animals must avoid extremely low or high temperatures.

The most commonly seen amphibians are frogs. Frogs live most everywhere, even here at Crater Lake National Park. They survive the winter by **hibernating,** which is like a long sleep, when they do not move or eat. Frogs can readily be heard during the spring when the males sing to attract females. Females are usually silent. Spring and summer are good times to explore the streams and ponds for frog eggs and tadpoles. **Remember**: Leave only footprints and take only pictures. Plants and animals may not be touched or taken from the park.

Life Cycle of a Frog: *Eggs are laid in water. Eggs hatch into tiny tadpoles. Back legs begin to grow. The gills disappear and tadpoles begin using lungs to breathe. Front legs begin to grow. The tail is fully absorbed into the body. The frog is ready to hop on land and become an adult frog.*

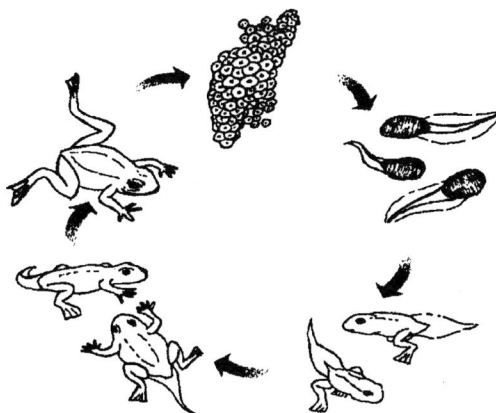

Pacific Tree Frog, *Pseudacris (Hyla) regilla*
Length: 1 to 1 7/8" long. Large head, a rounded snout, large eyes, a slim waist, and prominent toe pads. A jumper and a climber. Mature female is larger than the male. She has stripes on back and a triangle between her eyes. Both species have a dark stripe also along side of head. Male is light brown to dark brown with a V between eyes and 2 rows of large dark or bright green round spots on his back. Upper parts are smooth. **Habitat**: Grasslands, woodlands, forests, near water. **Voice**: High-pitched *kreck-ek.*

Where will you find me?

_____

Cascades Frog, *Rana cascadae*
Length: 1 3/4 to 3". A mountain frog usually found near water. Brown to olive-brown above with inky-black spots on back and dark spotting on legs. Yellow, orange-yellow, or yellow tan under and on under side of legs. Breeds March to mid-August. **Habitat**: Near ponds, creeks, and lakes in vegetation such as grasses and ferns. **Voice**: Low-pitched grating, chuckling sound; may call from under or above water.

What color am I?

_____

Reptiles

Reptiles, like amphibians, are cold-blooded animals and need the warmth of the sun to raise their internal temperature. Early in the day, you might see a snake warming itself on the rocks, a pond turtle resting on a log or in mudbanks, or a lizard resting on a log. Some reptiles are active during the day and keep moving from sunny places to shady spots. Some reptiles you may see while at Crater Lake National Park are the northern alligator lizard, short-horned lizard, western skink, racer, common garter snake, and rubber boa. **Instructions**: Below are pictures of reptiles you might see while visiting Crater Lake National Park. Unscramble the names of the reptiles below. The scientific name is listed below each animal. **Hint**: If you need help unscrambling a name, look up the scientific name on the Amphibian & Reptile Checklist on page 48.

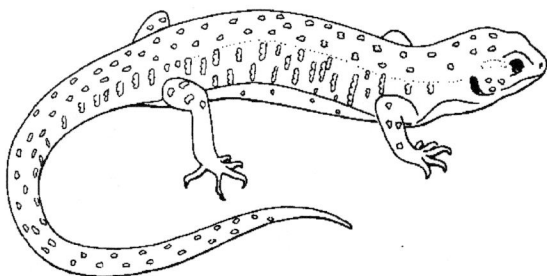

NERTHORN ROTAGILLA ZARDLI

Elgaria coerulea
Grey, olive, greenish, or bluish above with dark stripes on upper body.

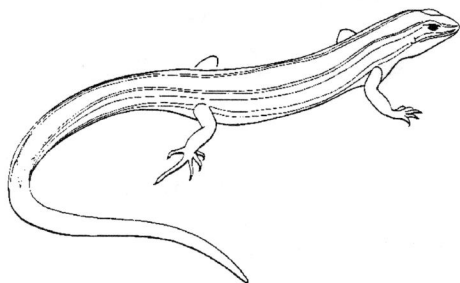

HSURBEGAS ZARDLI

Sceloporus graciosus
Grey or dark brown with blue patches on the each side of belly.

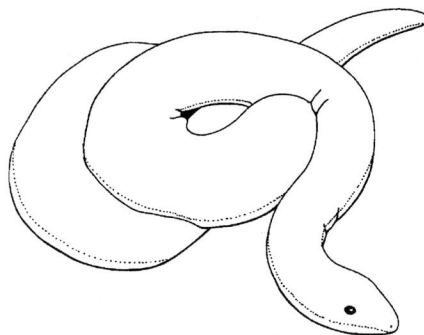

NERTWES ISKNK

Eumeces skitonianus
Dark brown above and light below. A light strip is bordered with black stripe.

REBBUR AOB

Charina bottae
Plain brown above, yellowish below.

TROHS-DENORH DARZIL

Phrynosoma douglassee
Brown or bluish gray above, dark spots, and sides and short tail edged with pinkish-white spines.

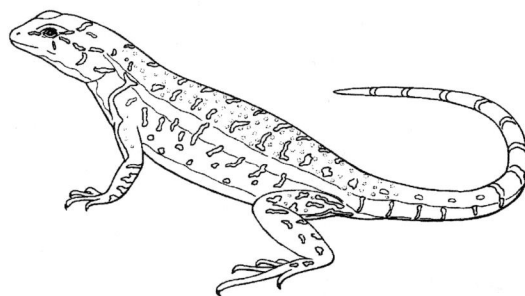

Fish in Crater Lake

Between 1888 and 1942, 1.8 million rainbow trout and kokanee salmon were introduced to Crater Lake. In 1888, William Gladstone Steel and his friends first lowered the fish down to the lake in buckets. The practice of stocking the lake continued until 1942. Today, the amount of food (plankton) in the lake determines the size of the population of fish. When food is plentiful, so are large numbers of fish. In 2007, the number of fish in the lake is low because in 2006 trout and salmon in the lake depleted their food resources.

Fish in Crater Lake eat amphipods, daphnia, midges, caddisflies, mayflies, beetles, bees, ants, moths, leeches, worms, snails, and blue-green and green filamentous algae.

____ **Rainbow Trout,** *Onchorhynchus mykiss*
____ **Kokanee Salmon,** *Onchorhynchus nerka*

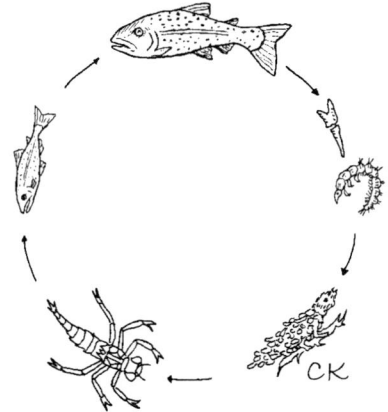

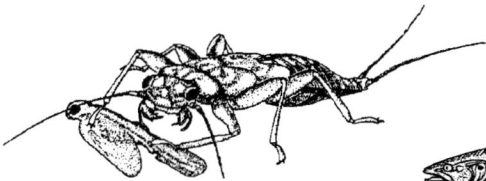

Stone fly eating a trout hatchling.

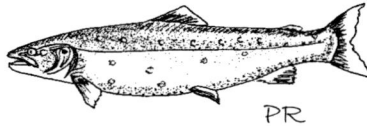

Kokanee Salmon, *Onchorhynchus nerka*
A landlocked sockeye salmon.

Example of a fish food web.

Plankton in Crater Lake

An important part of Crater Lake food chain is plankton. Both phytoplankton (plant) and zooplankton (animal) are an essential food supply for the animals that live in or visit the lake.

Phytoplankton: diatoms and dinoflagellates are microscopic algae and a major food source for animals of the lake. **Zooplankton:** The microscopic copepods and the larval stages of many larger zooplankton are the major consumers of phytoplankton and smaller zooplankton. Plankton provide a vital food source for the fish, frogs, toads, salmanders, and other animals growing in and near the lake. Shown below are some of the plankton in the lake.

Phytoplankton

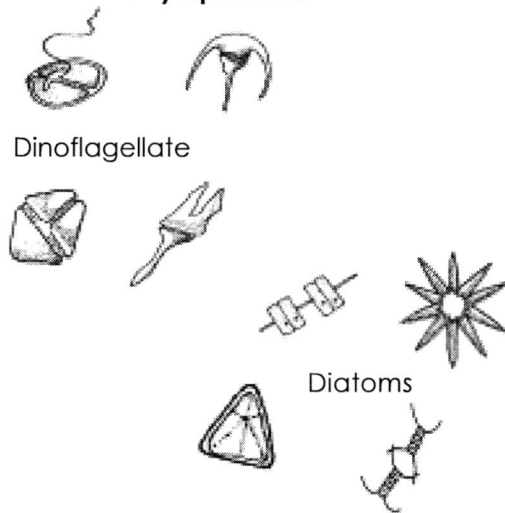

Dinoflagellate

Diatoms

Zooplankton

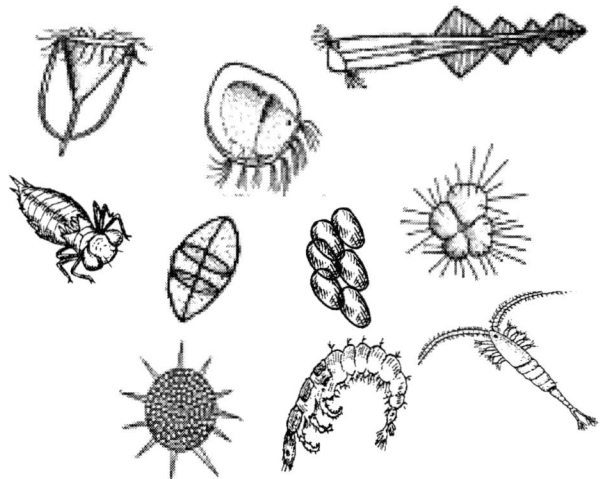

Aquatic Insects

Aquatic insects are an important part of the food chain in wetland areas. Dragonflies eat the pesky mosquitos. Larvae, nymphs and adult insects are food for birds and animals living in or visiting the lake, ponds, creeks, and meadows at Crater Lake National Park.

About 5,000 insect species in North America spend part or all of their lives in the water. Water beetles, for example, spend their entire lives in the water. Other insects, such as dragonflies, only spend the first part of their lives in the water. Aquatic insects have special adaptations, a characteristic that helps them survive in a certain environment. The water strider, pictured below, has dense, water-resistant hairs covering segments of its legs that trap tiny air bubbles to help keep it afloat.

A water strider walking on water.

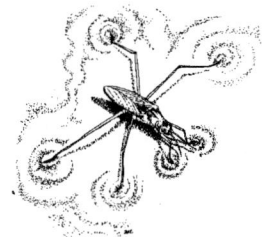

Insects develop through a process called metamorphosis - a change in form. Below are illustrations of complete and incomplete metamorphosis. A caddisfly begins its life as an egg, grows into two separate larvae stages before entering the pupa phase. The adult emerges from the pupa. **This process is complete metamorphosis**. A dragonfly lays its eggs on emergent vegetation. The egg develops into a nymph. The adult dragonfly emerges from the nymph, leaving the exoskelton on the aquatic or emergent plant. **This process is called incomplete metamorphosis**. Some aquatic insects, when they reach the adult stage, emerge from the water. Below the metamorphosis cycles are a list of aquatic insects under either the complete or incomplete metamorphis category.

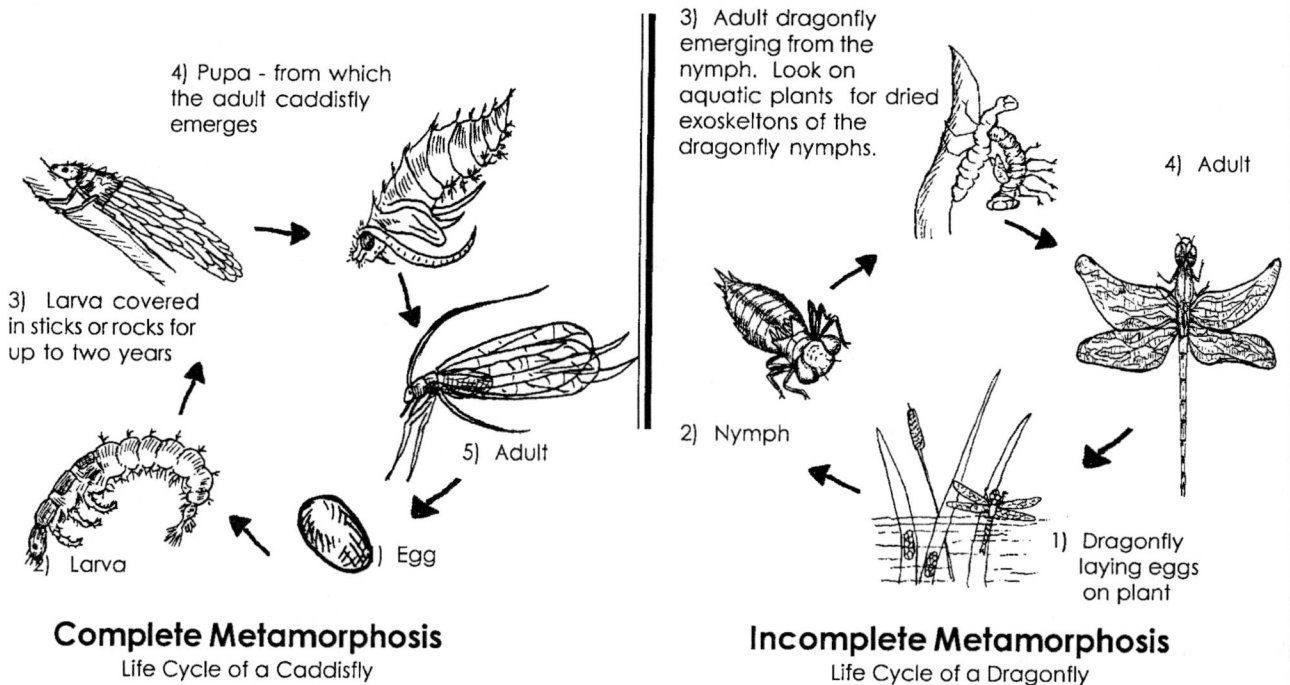

4) Pupa - from which the adult caddisfly emerges

3) Larva covered in sticks or rocks for up to two years

5) Adult

2) Larva

1) Egg

3) Adult dragonfly emerging from the nymph. Look on aquatic plants for dried exoskeltons of the dragonfly nymphs.

4) Adult

2) Nymph

1) Dragonfly laying eggs on plant

Complete Metamorphosis
Life Cycle of a Caddisfly

Incomplete Metamorphosis
Life Cycle of a Dragonfly

Caddisfly   Mosquito

Cranefly

Dragonfly   Water Beetle

Mayfly   Stonefly

Insects of Crater Lake National Park

The insect world includes some of the most fascinating creaures on earth. More than 925,000 species inhabit the earth, and they range in size from microscopic to several inches long. Many exhibit dazzling, bright color patterns. Many insects are essential for plant reproduction, as they carry pollen from one plant to another. Some insects can be harmful to crops and trees in a forest.

Insects are present in virtually every habitat. The more places you look for them, the more you will see. On the Castle Crest Wildflower Trail (page 70) you may see beetles and other animals on or under downed or nursery logs, butterflies flitting from flower to flower, or dragonflies and aquatic insects along and in the creeks. Other areas you may see insects are along the rim, on trails, and wetland areas such as Crater Lake, bogs, creeks, and ponds. Sit quietly and you will see them.

Butterflies and moths are some of the most colorful insects. The primary difference between the two are the antennae. Butterflies have knobbed antennae and moths antennae are linear. Butterflies are diurnal and most moths are nocturnal. Some of the butterflies seen in the park are on the next page.

Life Cycle of the Pandora Moth

Pandora Moth, *Coloradia pandora*
Also called the Pine Moth. If you visit the Sinnott Memorial Overlook, you may see hundreds of pandora moths sleeping on the walls and ceiling of the parapet. The pandora moth has a two year cycle. In June of the first year, the female lays eggs on the branches and needles of ponderosa pine. The larvae remain on the tree over winter feeding on foliage. The following summer the pupa drop off the trees and find an area with moist soil to metamorphize into an adult moth. The moth larvae are brownish to yellowish green and about 1" long at maturity. The adult is brown-gray with black markings on its wings.

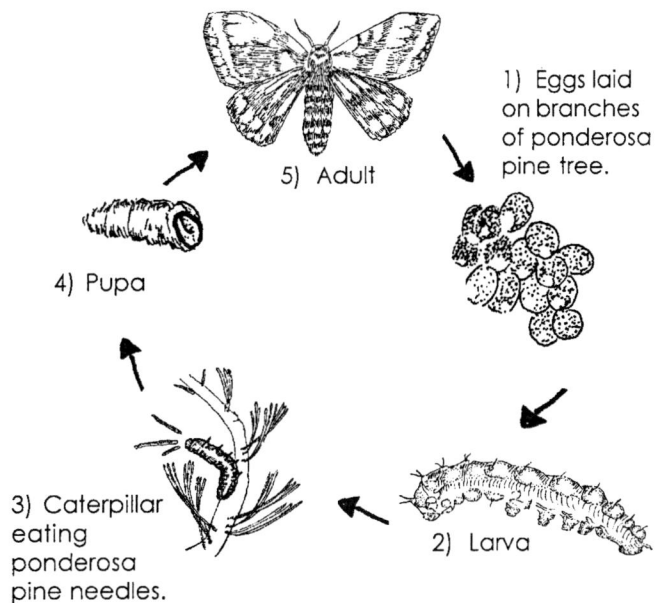

5) Adult

1) Eggs laid on branches of ponderosa pine tree.

4) Pupa

3) Caterpillar eating ponderosa pine needles.

2) Larva

White-lined Sphinx Moth, *Hyles lineata*
Wing span - 2 to 4". Upper wing is dark olive brown with paler tan along the middle line and edge, hindwing is black with reddish-pink middle band. Adults fly at dusk, during the night, and at dawn. Caterpillars grow in shallow burrows in the ground. **Diet**: Willow weed, evening primrose, and purslane. Adults eat nectar from columbines, larkspurs, penstemon, honeysuckle, thistles.

Life cycle of the pandora moth and the white sphinx moth by PR.

Butterflies of Crater Lake National Park

Often called "Painted Ladies," there are over 20,000 different species of butterflies worldwide. While visiting the park you may see a few that live in or visit Crater Lake National Park. Butterflies are beautiful and many adaptations help with their survival. The monarch butterfly tastes awful and birds have adapted to know not to eat them. The good tasting viceroy butterfly mimics the markings of the monarch butterfly and thereby is not prey for many birds. Plants depend on insects for pollination. As they flit from one plant to another they leave pollen, ensuring the plants will produce viable seeds. Place a checkmark next to the ones you see while visitng the park.

Instructions: Below are some of the butterflies you may see while visiting Crater Lake National Park. **Part I** - Unscramble the name of the butterfly and write its name on the line provided. **Part II** - Place the unscrambled underlined words in the puzzle.

INGNOURM KLOAC

Purplish-maroon wings, periwinkle spots, and yellow wing borders.

SUIDOLC SUISSANRAP

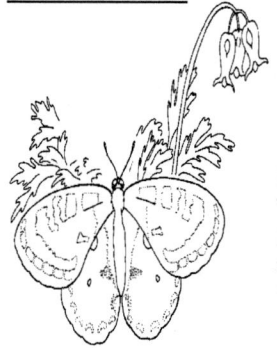

Milky white with black spots, red spots in central spots on hind wings.

SMILTERB ESOITROT LLEHS

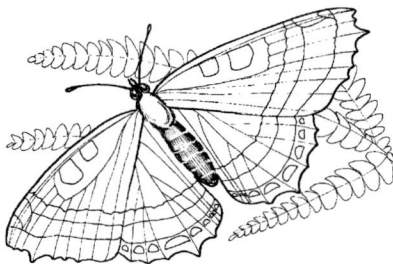

Blackish-brown wings with blue border spots, orange and yellow bands with red-orange spots at top of wings.

AINORFILAC ESIOTROT LLEHS

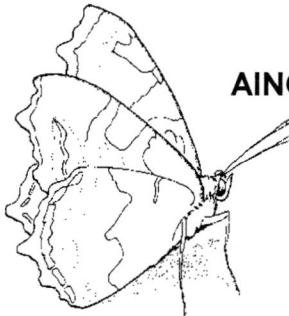

Orange-brown wings with black patches and borders and white spots near tips.

Checklist of Butterflies

_____Artic Blue
_____Biosduvall's Blue
_____California Tortoiseshell
_____Clodius Parnassius
_____Fritillary
_____Lorquin's Admiral
_____Mariposa Copper
_____Milbert's Tortoiseshell
_____Mourning Cloak
_____Northern Checkerspot
_____Painted Lady
_____Pine White
_____West Coast Lady
_____Western Tiger Swallowtail
_____Western White
_____Wood Nymph.

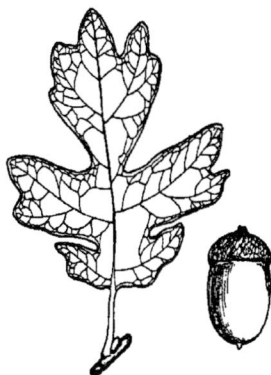

Oregon White Oak
Quercus garryana

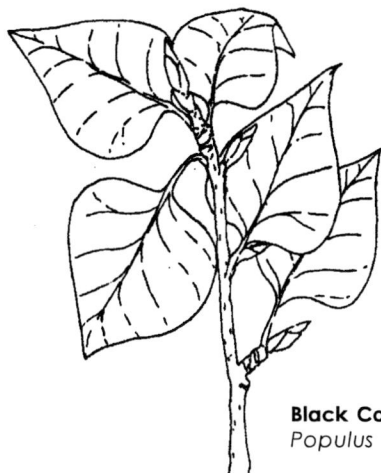

Black Cottonwood
Populus trichocarpa

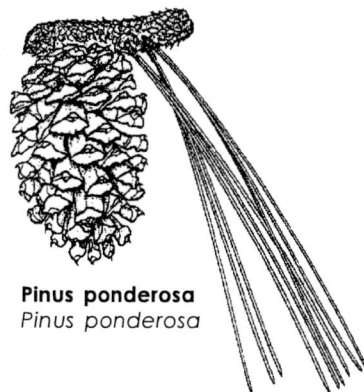

Pinus ponderosa
Pinus ponderosa

Plants of Crater Lake National Park

Page

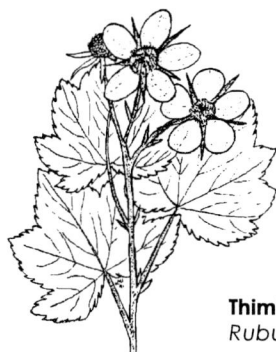

Thimbleberry
Rubus parviflorus

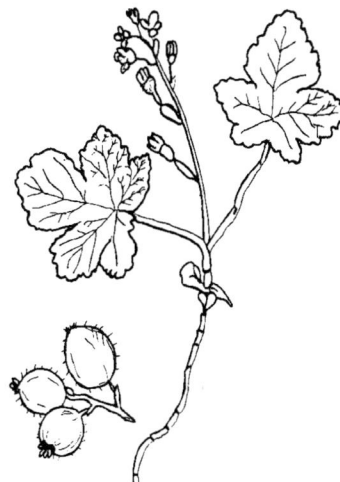

Crater Lake Currant
Ribes Erythrocarpum

Trees of Crater Lake National Park

A tree is a relatively tall, woody plant having great height and a single trunk, versus a shrub which is a low, woody plant having several stems, a bush.

Instructions: Part I - On the line provided next to each tree write in the date you saw it.   In your journal you can record more observations: location of the tree; which season (summer, spring, winter, or fall), weather conditions, or draw a picture of the tree and the area surrounding the tree.

The graceful whitebark pine tree is sculpted - gnarled and twisted - by disease, the harsh winter winds, and storms.

Big Leaf Maple
Acer macrophyllum
(dark green leaves)

Trees

Conifers

_____ **Douglas-fir** Pseudotsuga menziesii
_____ **Englemann Spruce** Picea engelmanii
_____ **Incense Cedar** Calocedrus decurrens
_____ **Lodgepole Pine** Pinus contorta
_____ **Mountain Hemlock** Tsuga mertensiana
_____ **Noble Fir** Abies procera
_____ **Ponderosa Pine** Pinus ponderosa
_____ **Shasta Fir** Abies shastensis
_____ **Subalpine Fir** Abies lasiocarpa
_____ **Sugar Pine** Pinus lambertiana
_____ **Western Hemlock** Tsuga heterophylla
_____ **Western White Pine** Pinus monticola
_____ **White Fir** Abies concolor
_____ **Whitebark Pine** Pinus albicaulis

Hardwoods

_____ **Big Leaf Maple** Acer macrophyllum
_____ **Black Cottonwood** Populus trichocarpa
_____ **Mountain Alder** Alnus tenuifolia
_____ **Mountain-ash** Sorbus scopulina
_____ **Oregon White Oak** Quercus garryana
_____ **Pacific Willow** Salix lucida lasiandra
_____ **Quaking Aspen** Populus tremuloides
_____ **Thinleaf Alder** Alnus incana

Incense Cedar
Calocedrus decurrens
(cone: reddish-brown
needles: dark green)

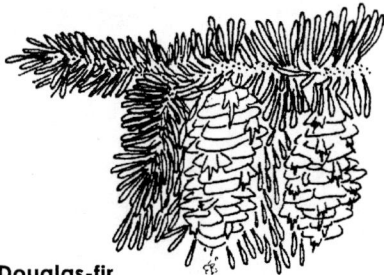

White Fir
 Abies concolor
(The cones sit on top of the branch. When the sun is shining behind the tree, the cones look like candles.)

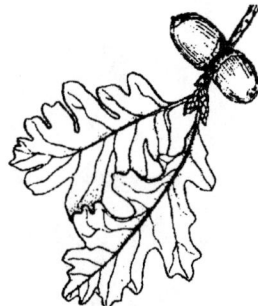

Douglas-fir
Pseudotsuga menziesii
(needles dark or bluish-green)

Oregon White Oak
Quercus garryana
(bright green leaves,
acorn: dark brown cap, tan body)

-56-

Shrubs of Crater Lake National Park

Instructions: Part I - On the line provided next to each plant write in the date you saw the shrub. In your journal record more observations: location of the shrub, which season (summer, spring, winter, or fall), weather conditions, draw a picture of the shrub, describe the area surrounding the shrub, and any animals that may be visiting the shrub.

Elliptical

Heart-shaped

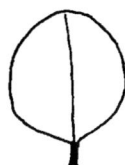

Rounded

Oval

Palmately Lobed

Pinnately Lobed

Narrow

Lance-shaped

Oblong

Wedge

Shrubs Checklist

_____ **Alpine Bog Kalmia** *Kalmia microphylla*
_____ **Antelope Bitterbrush** *Purshia tridentala*
_____ **Baldhip Rose** *Rosa gymnocarpa*
_____ **Bearberry Honeysuckle** *Lonicera involucrata*
_____ **Bitter Cherry** *Prunus emarginata*
_____ **Cascades Mahonia (Oregon Grape)** *Mahonia nervosa*
_____ **Cliff Penstemon** *Penstemon rupicola*
_____ **Crater Lake Currant** *Ribes erythrocarpum*
_____ **Cream Mountainheath** *Phyllodoce glanduliflora*
_____ **Creeping Raspberry** *Rubus lasiococcus*
_____ **Creeping Snowberry** *Symphoricarpos mollis*
_____ **Davidson Penstemon** *Penstemon davidsonii*
_____ **Douglas Rocky Mountain Maple** *Acer glabrum douglasii*
_____ **Dwarf Blueberry** *Vaccinium cespitosum*
_____ **Fremont Silktassel (Bearbrush)** *Garrya fremontii*
_____ **Golden Chinkapin** *Castanopsis chrysophylla*
_____ **Gray Rabbitbrush** *Ericameria nauseosus*
_____ **Greenleaf Manzanita** *Arctostaphylos patula*
_____ **Grouse Whortleberry** *Vaccinium scoparium*
_____ **Lewis Mockorange** *Philadelphus lewisii*
_____ **Oceanspray** *Holodiscus microphyllus*
_____ **Paific Serviceberry** *Amelanchier utahensis*
_____ **Partridgefoot** *Luetkea pectinata*
_____ **Pinemat Manzanita** *Arctostaphylos nevadensis*
_____ **Piper Mahonia** *Mahonia aquifolium*
_____ **Prickly Currant** *Ribes lacustre*
_____ **Purple Honeysuckle** *Lonicera conjugialis*
_____ **Rabbitbrush Goldenweed** *Ericamejia bloomeri*
_____ **Shasta Knotweed** *Polygonum shastense*
_____ **Sitka Mountain Ash** *Sorbus sitchensis*
_____ **Spreading Phlox** *Phlox diffusa*
_____ **Squawcarpet Ceanothus** *Ceanothus prostratus*
_____ **Sticky Currant** *Ribes viscosissimun*
_____ **Supalpine Spirea** *Spiraea splendeus*
_____ **Torrey Rocky Mountain Maple** *Acer glabrum torreyi*
_____ **Wax Currant** *Ribes cereum*
_____ **Western Thimbleberry** *Rubus parviflorus*
_____ **Whitebark Raspberry** *Rubus leucodermis*
_____ **Willows** *Salix spp.*

Keying Out Trees

To identify the trees you see at Crater Lake or any natural area, you can use this simple key. **Instructions: Part I** - Key out the leaves of the trees illustrated on the next page. At each option, you have two choices. Select the one that best represents the leaf of the tree and go on to the next set of options until you have identified the tree. **Part II** - Write the name of the tree on the line below the picture of the leaf on the next page. Below the leaves are the scientific names to help you identify the tree.

1)   Tree is an **evergreen** (*does not lose its leaves in the winter*)   go to **2**
      Tree is **deciduous** (*loses its leaves in the winter*)   go to **3**

2)   Leaves are shaped like **needles**   Ponderosa Pine
      Leaves are **scale-like**   Incense Cedar

3)   Leaves are **simple**   go to **4**
      Leaves are **compound**   Mountain Ash

4)   Leaves are **opposite**   Big Leaf Maple
      Leaves are **alternate**   go to **5**

5)   Leaves are **thin & ovate** (*egg-shaped*)   Thinleaf Alder
      Leaves are **leaves are oblong to roundish**   Mountain Alder

Needles in bundles of 1 - 5 with papery sheaths surrounding the base.

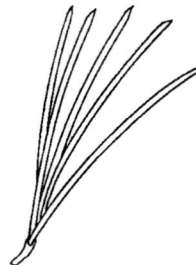

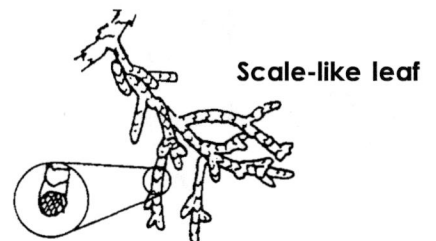

Scale-like leaf

Alternate leaves grow singly along the branch, with space between each leaf.

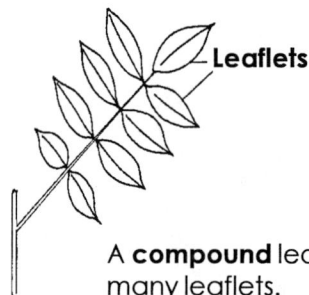

Leaflets

A **compound** leaf has many leaflets.

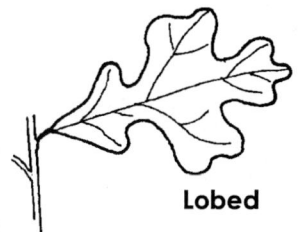

Lobed

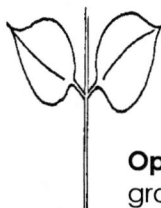

Opposite leaves grow directly across from one another, in pairs.

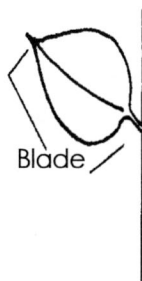

Blade

A **simple** leaf is made up of only one leaf blade.

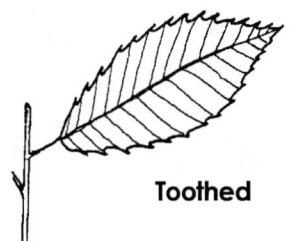

Toothed

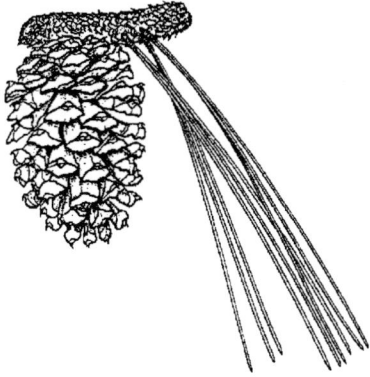

Pinus ponderosa

Acer macrophyllum

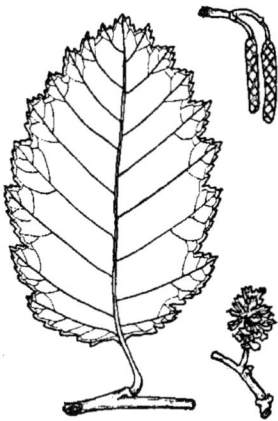

Quercus garryana

Alnus sinuata

Calocedrus decurrens

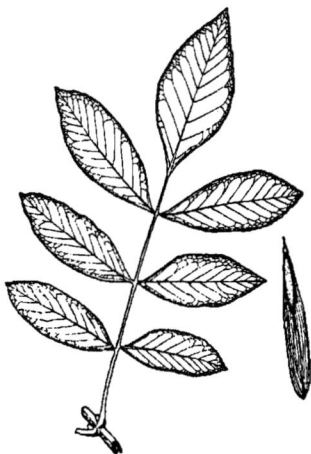

Sorbus scopulina

Populus trichocarpa

Whitebark Pine and Clark's Nutcracker

Whitebark Pine, *Pinus albicaulis*,

    The long, harsh **winters** at **Crater** Lake curtail the whitebark's growth. A limb, the size of a straw may represent 50 years of growth. Living 200 to 1,000 years, whitebark pines may grow to 100 feet tall in a valley forest or remain **gnarled** shrubs on ridges, whipped by fierce **alpine** winds. The whitebark pine is a vulnerable species: 1) it is dependant on the Clark's nutcracker to bury its seeds; 2) white pine **blister rust** (a fungus - *Cronartium ribicola)* from Eurasia is established in the park, and is infecting whitebark pine and other 5-needle pine trees. Its host plants are gooseberries and currants; and 3) porcupines feed on the bark or phloem (tube where nutrients are transported throughout the tree). If the phloem is severed, the tree can die. At lower elevations it is mixed in with mountain **hemlock**, Shasta fir, and western white pine. As elevation increases other species gradually drop out, leaving the whitebark pine alone on mountain slopes and ridges. You can see whitebark pine populations along the Rim Drive, on Mount Scott, and on **Wizard** Island. Some populations look like *ghost trees* - their silvery skeletons (dead limbs and trunks) twisted and gnarled shimmering in the afternoon sun.

    Whitebark pine cones do not open at maturity, so the seeds cannot fall out. The tree needs the Clark's nutcracker to open the cones and retrieve the seeds. Whitebark pine seeds are then buried by the Clark's nutcracker. While a small number of cones are opened by squirrels, the vast majority are efficiently opened by the **Clark's nutcracker**. They may collect **seeds** from several cones or trees before burying them in the ground. The cache site may be at the base of a tree or they may fly many miles away to bury their seeds. Seeds are buried about an inch below ground. **Caches** contain 1 - 15 seeds. Nutcrackers rely on memory to find their caches. The forgotten nutcracker caches may produce future stands of whitebark pine. Many other animals eat and **disperse** whitebark pine seeds, including American marten, golden-mantled **ground squirrels**, chipmunks, **deer** mice, and bears.

    <u>Height</u>: Six to 20 feet high on windswept ridges, up to 100 feet in protected forest valleys. <u>Leaves</u>: **Needles** in bundles of five, one to 1½" long, stiff, dark **green**. <u>**Cones**</u>: One to three inches long, very resinous, dark purple. <u>Seeds:</u> 1/3 - 1/2" long, wingless. <u>Habitat</u>: High mountains, at **timberline**, from 6,500 - 12,000'. <u>Edible</u>**:** The seeds are large, very nutritious, and flavorful. Native Americans used them for food, fresh or roasted, or mixed with **dried** berries and preserved for winter. <u>Tidbits</u>: For more information about the park's blister rust resource management project see pages 94 and 95.

*The very **survival** of the tree is dependant on the Clark's nutcracker to bury its seeds.*

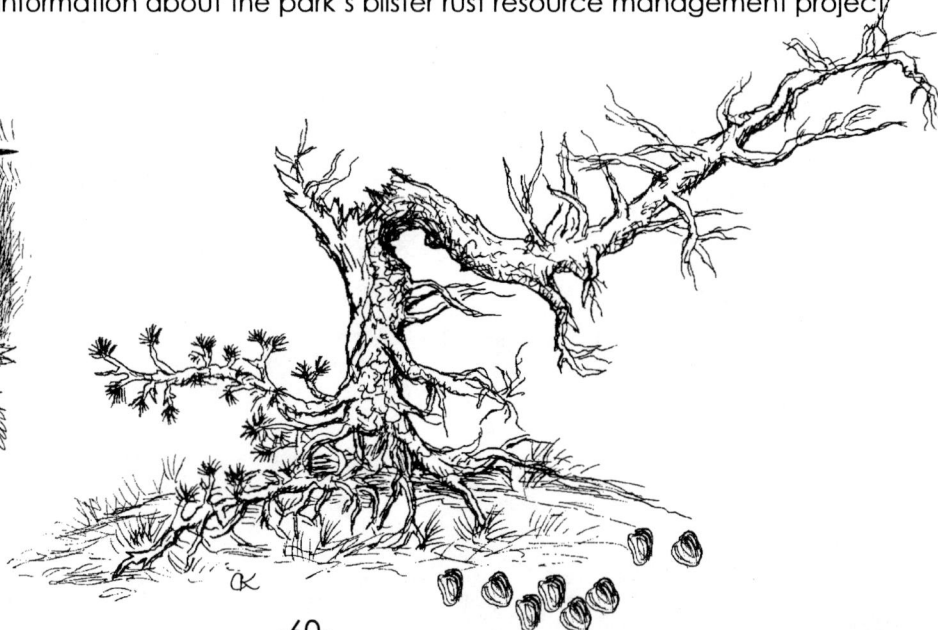

Whitebark Pine and the Clark's Nutcracker

Instructions: In the description of the whitebark pine tree are words in **bold** type. Place those words in the puzzle below. Letters of several words have been provided to start you out.

Whitebark Pine Cone

Whitebark Pine
Seedling

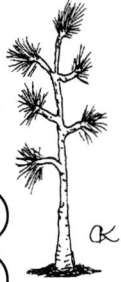

W

N

B

W

D

H

A

S

The **Clark's nutcracker** prying and pulling out seeds from the whitebark pine cone.

Whitebark pine needles - in bundles of 5.

-61-

Tree Rings Maze

Trees can't talk but they can tell you a lot about themselves if you know what to look for. You can learn a lot about the life of a tree by reading its rings. Reading tree rings and tree scars can tell you the history of the tree. Has the tree been in a fire, experienced drought, or has an insect drilled a hole in the bark and laid its eggs?

Instructions: **Part I** - Enter the maze and make your way to the center ring. How old is the tree? Count the number of rings and place your answer on this line. _____

Part II - How many scars and holes can you did you see as you made your way to the center of the ring? _____ Do you see any holes drilled by a woodpecker? _____

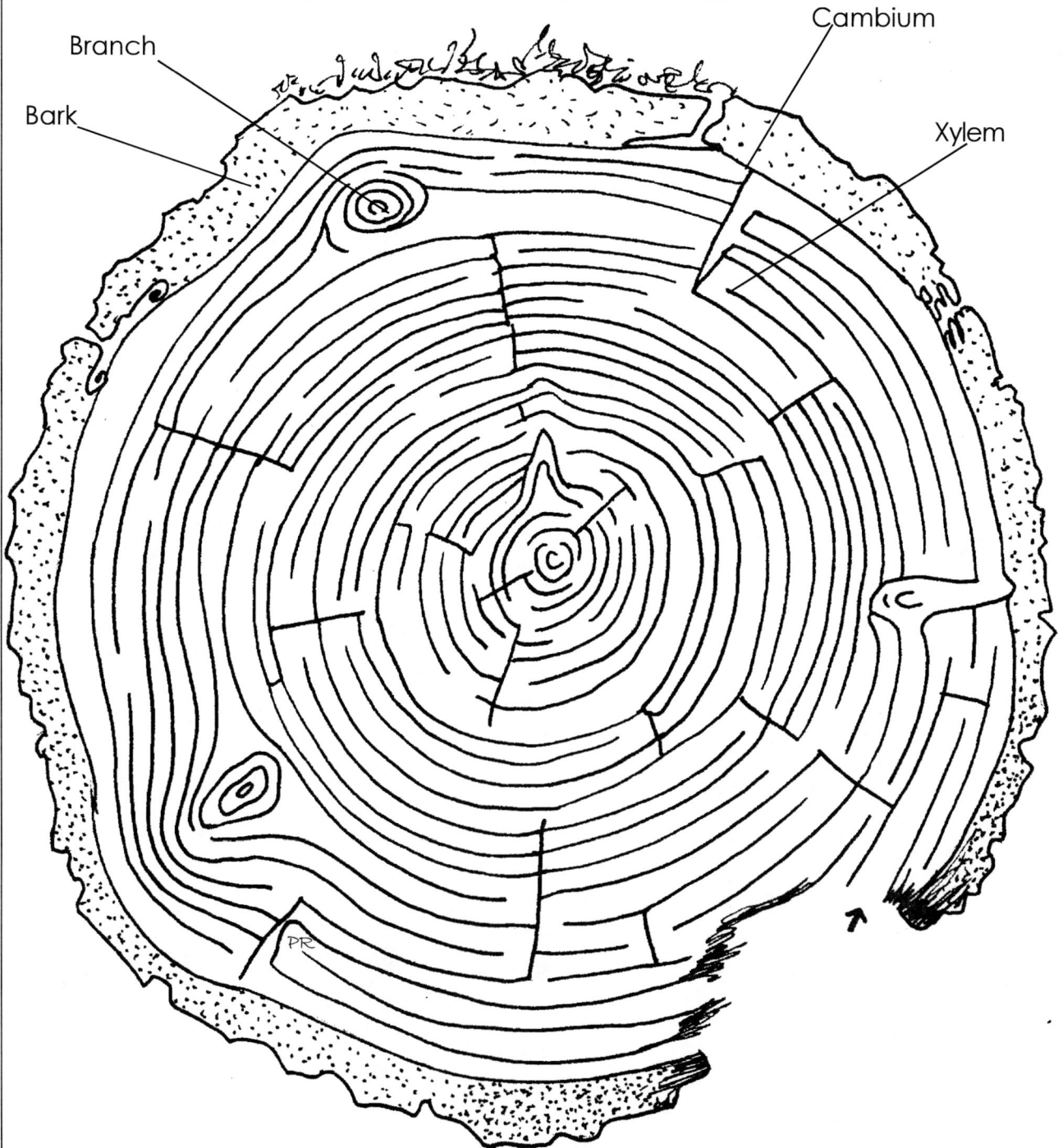

Cambium

Branch

Bark

Xylem

Herbs of Crater Lake National Park
Wildflowers

Spring comes late at Crater Lake National Park. The park elevation ranges from 4,000' to over 8,000'. All summer long you can enjoy wildflowers. They start blooming in June at the lower elevations, especially at the Panhandle (page 82), Annie Creek (page 68), Castle Crest Wildflower Trail (page 70), Vidae Falls, stops along Rim Drive, Garfield Peak, and around the Steel Visitor Center at Park Headquarters. For example, compare the monkeyflower growing at Castle Crest Wildflower Trail with the ones growing at the Grotto Cover Overlook on Rim Drive. Are they the same size? _____ Are they blooming at the same time?_____ The higher up you drive or hike, the later they bloom, all the way through August. The higher up in elevation, such as Dutton Creek Trail, Watchman Lookout Trail, or Mount Scott, the flowers may be smaller because they have a shorter growing period as the snow melts later than at Annie Creek or in the Panhandle. Below is a checklist of some of the wildflower you may see. Over the next three pages, some of the wildflowers are illustrated to help you identify some of the more than one hundred flowers in the park.

Instructions: On the line provided next to each herb write in the date you saw it. In your journal you can record more observations: location of the wildflower; which season (summer, spring, winter, or fall), weather conditions, or draw a picture of the wildflower and the area surrounding the flower. Is there a creek nearby?

____**Alpine Buckwheat** *Eriogonum pyrolifolium*
____**Alpine Shootingstar** *Dodecatheon alpinum*
____**American Bistort** *Polygonum bistortoides*
____**American False Hellebore** *Veratrum viride*
____**Anderson's Lupine** *Lupinus andersonii*
____**Applegates' Paintbrush** *Castilleja applegatei*
____**Arrowleaf Groundsel** *Senecio triangularis*
____**Blue Stickseed** *Hackelia milsantha*
____**Cascade Aster** *Aster ledophyllus*
____**Columbia Monkshood** *Aconitum columbianum*
____**Common Cow Parsnip** *Heracleum maximum*
____**Common Pearly Everlasting** *Anaphalis margaritacea*
____**Common Yellow Monkeyflower** *Mimulus guttatus*
____**Cobwebby Paintbrush** *Castilleja arachnoidoa*
____**Crater Lake Violet** *Viola adunca*
____**Creamy Stonecrop** *Sedum oregonese*
____**Davidson's Penstemon** *Penstemon davidsonii*
____**Dwarf Hulsea** *Hulsea nana*
____**Dwarf Monkeyflower** *Mimulus nanus*
____**Elephanthead Pedicularis** *Pedicularis groenlandica*
____**Fireweed** *Epilobium angustifolium*
____**Goldenrod** *Solidago canadensis*
____**Goosefoot or Mountain Violet** *Viola purpurea*
____**Green Corn Lily** *Veratrum viride*
____**Hot Rocks Penstemon** *Penstemon deustus*
____**Jessica's Stickseed** *Hackella micrantha*
____**Lanceleaf Spring Beauty** *Claytonia lanceolata*

____**Lewis' Monkeyflower** *Mimulus lewisii*
____**Longleaf Arnica** *Arnica longifolia*
____**Newberry's Knotweed** *Polygonum newberryi*
____**Nodding Microseris** *Microseris nutaus*
____**Orange Agoseris** *Agoseris aurantiaca*
____**Pacific Bleeding Heart** *Dicentra formosa*
____**Pioneer Violet** *Viola glabella*
____**Prairie Lupine** *Lupinus lepidus var. sellulus*
____**Primrose Monkeyflower** *Mimulus primuloides*
____**Pussy Paws** *Calyptridum umbellatum*
____**Queencup Beadlily** *Clintonia uniflora*
____**Rabbitbrush Goldenweed** *Esicameria bloomeri*
____**Rock Penstemon** *Penstemon rupicola*
____**Scarlet Paintbrush** *Castilleja miniata*
____**Silverleaf Phacelia** *Phacelia hastata*
____**Sitka or Crimson Columbine** *Aquilegia formosa*
____**Sitka Valerian** *Valeriana sitchensis*
____**Sky Rocket Gilia** *Ipomopsis aggregata*
____**Snowbush Ceanothus** *Ceanothus velutinus*
____**Spreading Phlox** *Phlox diffusa*
____**Sticky Cinquefoil** *Potentilla glandulosa*
____**Subalpine Spirea** *Spiraea densiflora*
____**Tolmie's Saxifrage** *Saxifraga tolmiei*
____**Western Pasqueflower** *Anemone occidentalis*
____**Woodland Pinedrops** *Pterospora andromedea*
____**Wooly Sunflower** *Eriophyllum lanatum*
____**Yellow Fawn Lily** *Erythronium grandiflorum*
____**Yellow-staining Collomia** *Collomia tinctoria*

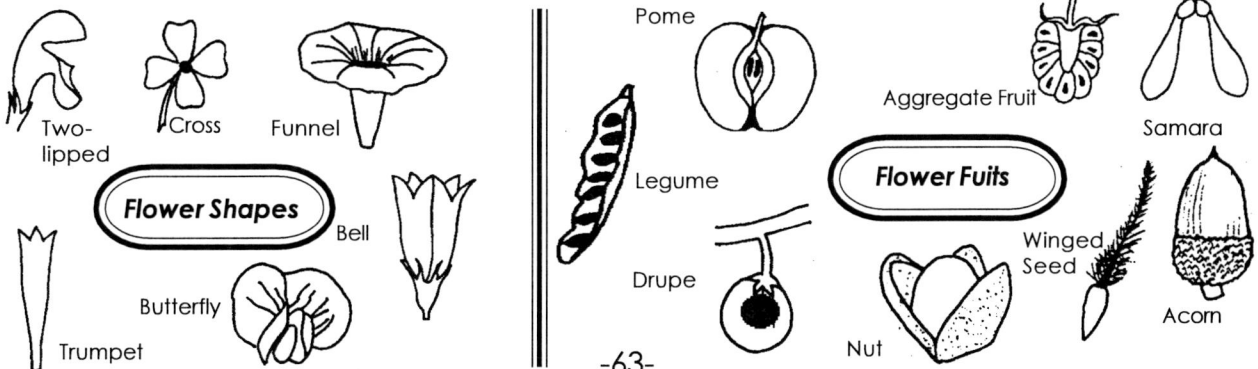

Flower Shapes: Two-lipped, Cross, Funnel, Bell, Butterfly, Trumpet

Flower Fuits: Pome, Aggregate Fruit, Samara, Legume, Drupe, Nut, Winged Seed, Acorn

Wildflowers of Crater Lake National Park

From June through August, the forests, meadows, trails, falls, and creeks are alive with color. Wildflowers fill the cliffsides with thousands of penstemon, paintbrush, violets, gilia, and many other wildflowers. One of the best places to see many flowers is the Castle Crest Wildflower Trail (see page 70). **Instructions:** As you walk around the park, if you see a plant illustrated below and on pages 65 and 66, put a ✔ in the box next to the wildflower. As you identify a plant, use crayons or colored pencils to color it and its name. For example, the flower of the scarlet paintbrush is red. Color the flowers, and when you have finished coloring it, find its name and color it red. **Hint:** If you need help in identifying the wildflowers below, refer to the Wildflowers Checklist on page 63.

Red
Yellow
Yellowish-orange

☐ **Penstemon davidsonii**
Flower: Blue-lavender to purple
Leaves: Dark Green

☐ **Ipomopsis aggregata**
Flower: Scarlet, spotted with yellow

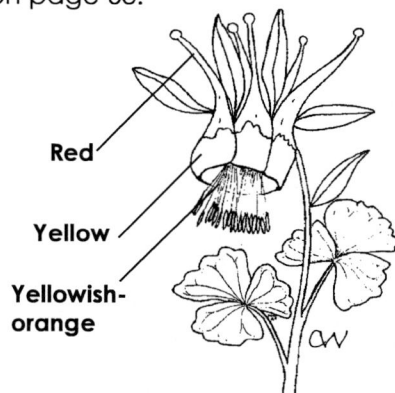

☐ **Aquilegia formosa**
Flower: Red, yellow, yellowish-orange

Yellow Fawn Lily

Pacific Bleeding Heart

Common Yellow Monkeyflower

Queencup Beadlily

Orange Agoseris

Sitka Columbine

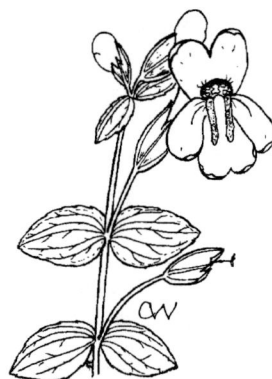

Sky Rocket Gilia

Davidson's Pensteman

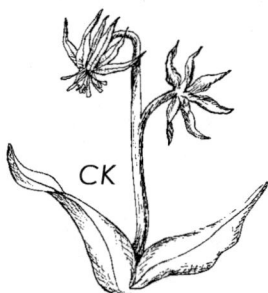

☐ **Agoseris aurantiaca**
Flower: Orange with red-orange center

☐ **Mimulus guttatus**
Flower: Yellow with orange center.

☐ **Erythronium grandiflorum**
Flower: Yellow

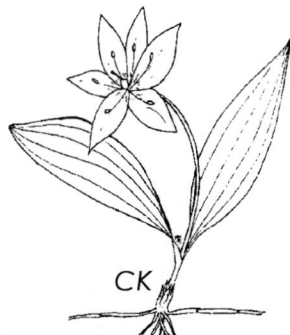

☐ **Clintonia uniflora**
Flower: White

☐ **Dicentra formosa**
Flower: Pink

Wildflowers of Crater Lake National Park

Bract ———————————— Flower

☐ **Western Pasqueflower**
Anemone occidentalis
Flower: White to purple

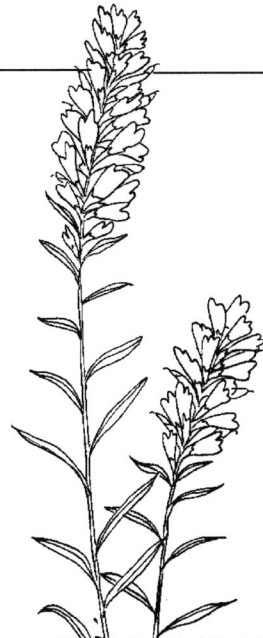

☐ **Scarlet Paintbrush**
Castilleja miniata
Bracts: Red
Flowers:
Yellowish-green

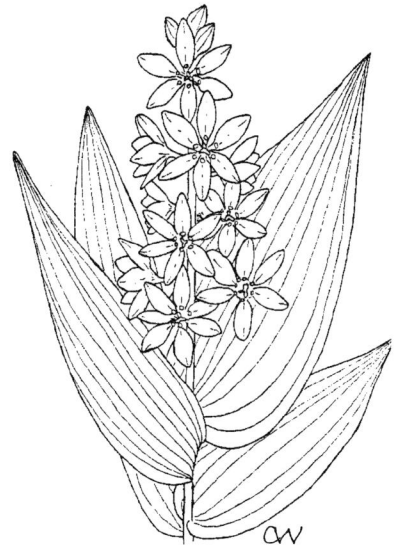

☐ **Common Pearly Everlasting**
Anaphalis margaritacea
Leaves: Greenish above, white below
Flower: Yellow, dry pearly white

☐ **Anderson's Lupine**
Lupinus andersonii
Flower: Blue to purple or white

☐ **American False Hellebore**
Veratrum viride
Leaves: Grayish-green
Flower: White with yellow centers

Wildflowers of Crater Lake National Park

☐ **Alpine Shooting Star**
Dedecatheon sp.
Flower: Purplish-pink with yellow band and dark tip

☐ **Lanceleaf Spring Beauty**
Claytonia lanceolata
Flower: White with yellow center

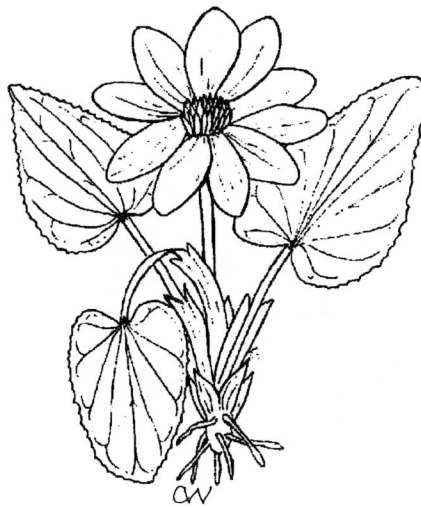

☐ **Marsh Marigold**
Caltha biflora
Flower: White with yellow centers.

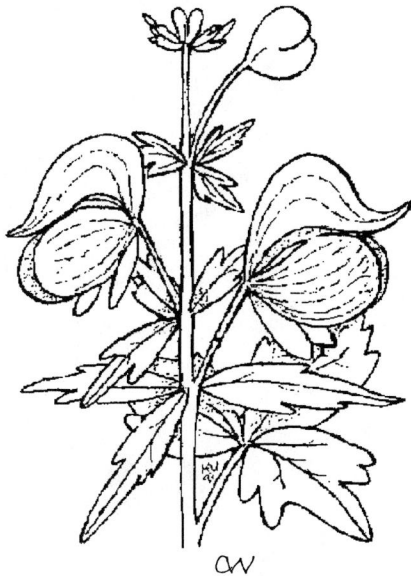

☐ **Columbia Monkshood**
Aconitum columbianum
Flower: Dark purple to blue, white, or yellow-green
Leaves: Dark green

☐ **Fireweed**
Epilobium angustifolium
Flower: Deep pink to magenta

A variety of insects, spiders, reptiles, and small mammals may live in or feed off of a downed or nursery log.

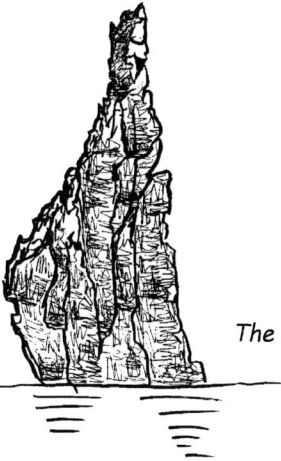

The Lady of the Lake sits in front of the Grotto.

Special Places at Crater Lake National Park

In this section, you will learn about 7 special places or habitats - a place where an animal or plant lives. Habitats provide food, water, shelter (protection from predators). Habitats can be as large as mountains or grasslands, as small as tidepools, or even a drop of water. There are many more special places in the Park and on each visit you can explore different areas of the Park. Other special areas to explore include Boundary Springs, headwaters of the Rogue River, and Llao Hallway (To visit this site, please to not go alone and wear a plastic helmet) to name just a few.

Annie Creek

As you walk through the forested area and along the adjacent Annie Creek banks you are in a riparian woodland. If you sit quietly by the creek you may see a belted kingfisher diving for a fish or an American dipper slipping underwater to search for aquatic insects. Or you may see animals or the tracks of a blacktail deer, black bear, marmot, long-tail weasel, porcupine, golden-mantled ground squirrels, and gray foxes. Or perhaps the track of a vole, mouse, or shrew at the creek's edge seeking fresh water or aquatic invertebrates or fish. Dawn or dusk are the best times to see most animals. Refer to *Animal Field Guide* pages 38 and 39 or *Mammal Key* on page 37 for help in identifying animal tracks. At various places along the trail or from Annie Creek viewing stops on Highway 62 you can see pinnacles, water falls, and meadows that are part of Annie Creek Canyon.

The creek is named in honor of Annie Gaines of Fort Klamath, who came to see Crater Lake on October 9, 1865 along with Mrs. O. T. Brown. They descended the walls to reach the Lake and touch the clear, blue water. Annie was the first white woman to touch the water. **Directions:** The Annie Creek Trail can be reached by driving to the Mazama Campground, the first right turn after enter the park from the south entrance. Follow directions to the Amphitheater. The beginning of the Trail is behind the Amphitheater. **Instructions:** Color the picture of Annie Creek. Circle the American dipper and draw in some of the animals you might see along the banks and in the creek.

Annie Creek

From a cascade frog to a butterfly, dragonfly to the American dipper bobbing in Annie Creek, this riparian woodland is a treasure chest just waiting to be discovered. As you walk along the trail or sit by the creek, what do you observe? In your journal draw or write down the names of the plants and animals you see at Annie Creek.

Instructions: Hidden in the nest puzzle below are some of the plants, animals, and natural & geological features of Annie Creek. Words in **bold** can be found forward, backwards, up, down, or diagonally.

American **Dipper**
Ancient **Fumerole**
Belted **Kingfisher**
Black **Bear**
Blue Butterfly
Caddisfly **Larvae**
Crayfish

Deer
Downed **Log**
Douglas-fir
Falls
Lady **Fern**
Marmot
Meadow

Monkeyflower
Moss
Mountain Hemlock
Nymph
Pinnacles
Pumice
Red Fir

Red **Fox**
Scarlet Paintbrush
Skyrocket **Gilia**
Tadpoles
White-headed **Bistort**
Willow
Winter Wren

Winter Wren
Troglodytes troglodytes

Douglas-Fir
Pseudotsuga menziesii

```
              W O L L I W
        F B I S T O R T F   B M
          U L A R V A E E L O O
          S B M R E D R E U N R U
    E T L E   E P N R E K   I N H
    C E L A L O R A   E T W F T S
    I L A R L C K O Y   O I S A I
    M R F E M C A F L D M N A I F
    U A S O I I L N A E R T L N Y
    P C S H L O G E N E A E G Y A
    S C I W   M   P I M R U M R
    G E X O F P   P   O P C
    R E H S I F G N I K D H
          D E E R
```

Mayfly Nymph
Order: *Ephemeroptera*

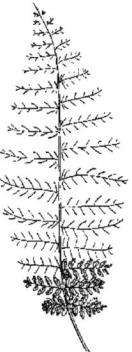

Lady Fern
Athyrium filix-femina

Mule Deer
Odocoileus hemionus

Pumice

Caddisfly & Larvae
Order: Trichoptera

Black Bears
Ursus americanus

Castle Crest Wildflower Trail

The Castle Crest Wildflower Trail encompasses two ecosystems - the forest and a riparian wetland area. Water from springs cascades down the cliff and creates lush vegetation in the summer. The meadows are filled with a variety of wildflowers - mountain violets, arrowleaf groundsel, common pearly-everlasting, purple asters, and blue stickseed. You may see a white-lined sphinx moth (see page 53) on a penstemon. More flowers and trees are listed in the Castle Crest Wildflower Trail Word Search. As you walk along the trail you may see downed logs or nursery logs. These logs play host to a variety of animals that live in or under the tree. Just under the bark you may see ants, sow bugs, beetles, worms, spiders. Under the tree live small rodents, lizards, and other animals. Some downed logs act as nursery logs. On nursery logs grow a variety of trees, lichen, and moss. **Directions:** To reach the Trail you can walk across the road from the Steel Visitor Center, or you can drive to the entrance on East Rim Drive. After leaving the parking lot at Steel Visitor Center, take a right turn, and then take a left turn onto East Rim Dirve. Just a few hundred feet after turning left, you will see the sign for the parking lot. **Instructions**: As you color this page, how many different kinds of plants and animals do you see in the picture? _____

Castle Crest Wildflower Trail Word Search

Instructions: In the puzzle below are words associated with Castle Crest Wildflower Trail. Words in **bold** can be found forward, backwards, up, down, or diagonally. Circle the letters of the words. Write the uncircled letters on the line below. The uncircled letters spell the names of other wildflowers and plants you may see on the Wildflower Trail.

_____

American **Bistort**
Bear
Black-tailed **Deer**
Butterfly
Columbia **Monkshood**
Crater Lake Currant
Creek
Dragonfly
Elephanthead Pedicularis
Hermit **Thrush**

Lewis' **Monkeyflower**
Lodgepole **Pine**
Lupine
Mountain **Chickadee**
Mountain **Hemlock**
Nursery **Log**
Pacific Bleeding **Heart**
Pacific Red **Elder**
Pinemat **Manzanita**

Red **Fox**
Rufous **Hummingbird**
Scarlet **Gilia**
Scarlet **Paintbrush**
Shasta **Fir**
Shooting Star
Spreading **Phlox**
White Bog **Orchid**
Winter **Wren**

Dragonfly

Pacific Bleeding Heart
Dicentra fomosa

Lewis' Monkeyflower
Mimulus lewisii

```
M O N K S H O O D N O C E
A O B T R O T S I B R D E
N R N X O F W R L A E R D
Z C F K I R E E T R,A A A
A H W I E N L E L T O G K
N I W,N I Y R D S G I O C
I D C P O L F G R L M N I
T A R N A B N L I X F F H
A T E K U I U A O I T L C
T R E T T P N L R W B Y K
H A K O I E H T R C E U C
R E O N G P P,L B I A R O
U H E C O E L D E R R H L
S E N Y L F R E T T U B M
H U M M I N G B I R D S E
D A E H T N A H P E L E H
```

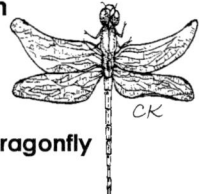

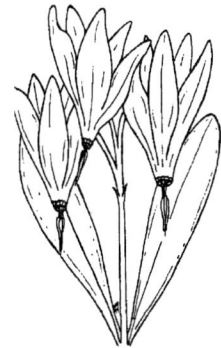

Alpine Shooting Star
Dodecatheon alpinum

Nursery Log

Mule Deer
Odocoileus hermionus

Castle Crest Wildflower Trail - Downed Log

A tree's life is not over when it falls down and becomes a log on the forest floor. Not only does the log provide a home and hiding place for many animals, but as it decays the log returns important nutrients to the soil, which feed the new plants and trees that grow to replace the fallen tree.

The downed or rotting log is home and nursery for beetles, worms, crustaceans, crickets, sow bugs, millipedes and centepedes, mites, spiders, ants, snakes, salamanders, newts, and chipmunks. Fungi and various molds help reduce the log to spongy fibers which becomes the perfect seedbed for plants. When new plants are growing on the downed log it is often called a nursery log.

Instructions: As you walk the Castle Crest Wildflower Trail look for a downed log, a nearby creek, or a meadow filled with wildflowers. In the box below, draw a picture of something you really like - a wildflower visited by a hummingbird, a butterfly flitting from flower to flower, a downed log with a variety of insects living in it, or your friends or family admiring a wildflower.

Castle Crest Wildflower Trail Birds

American Robin, *Turdus migratorius*
Large and sturdy with long legs and fairly long tail. Orange to red breast, yellow bill, lower white belly, and grayish back and head. **Length**: 10". **Wingspan**: 17". **Weight**: 2 3/4 oz.
Habitat: Coniferous forests, grassy lawns, tundra. **Call**: *Plurri, kiiwi or puk, puk or shheerr.* **Diet**: Earthworms, insects, snails, berries and other fruits. **Breeding Displays**: Males chase female, male struts around female with tail spread, wings shaking, throat inflated. **Nest**: Conifers, orchard trees, buildings, shrubs, cup shaped nest of mud, twigs and grass lined with fine grass. **Eggs**: 2 - 5, pale blue spotted with brown.

How much do I weigh?

_____

Hermit Thrush, *Cathasus guttatus*
Stocky, short-winged, upper body parts brown-olive to gray-brown, breast buffy or whitish, reddish tail and white eye-ring. **Length**: 6 3/4". **Wingspan**: 11 1/2". **Weight**: 1.1 oz. **Habitat**: Coniferous forests or mixed woodlands, thickets.
Call: *Freediila, fridla-fridla, chuck,* or *cheedila chli-chli-chli.* **Diet**: Spiders, earthworms, fruit. **Breeding Displays**: Wing flicking, sleek erect posture with bill pointed upward. **Nest**: On ground or low in decidu-ous or coniferous tree, made of weeds, rotted wood, twigs, grass, moss, mud, lining with fine materi-als. **Eggs**: 3 - 6, greenish-blue.

Name 3 foods I eat.

_____

Yellow-rumped Warbler, *Dendroica cornata*
Gray head, yellow throat, wide white patch on the wings, yellow rump, yellow patch on crown, and yellow patch at front of wings. **Length**: 5 1/2 - 6".
Wingspan: 8 1/2 - 9 1/4". **Weight**: 0.43 oz.
Habitat: Coniferous forests and mixed woodlands.
Call: Song is a soft warble, *sidl, sidl, sidl, sidl, seedl, seedl, seedl, seedl;* call is a low-pitched *chwit.* **Diet**: insects, berries. **Breeding Displays**: Courting male follows female, fluffs side feathers, raises wings, erects crownfeathers.
Nest: Usually on horizontal branch, made of shredded bark, weed stalks, twigs , lined with feathers and other materials. **Eggs**: 3 - 5, white to creamy.

What are my calls?

_____

American Dipper *Cinclus mexicanus*
Also called Water Ouzel. Stocky with short cocked tail and long legs. Dark grey. **Length**: 7 1/2 - 7 3/4". **Wingspan**: 11". **Weight**: 2 oz. **Habitat**: Clear rushing, rocky streams, as high as timberline. Can be seen bobbing up and down in streams, walks under water. **Call**: *K-tee k-tee wif-if-if-if treeoo treeoo tsbri tsbri tsbri tsbri.* **Diet**: Aquatic insects, occasionally small fish or fish eggs. **Breeding Displays**: Male stretches neck upward, bill vertical, wings down and partly spread, struts and sings to female. **Nest**: On cliff face among moss and ferns, behind waterfalls, or on mid-stream rocks; nest of moss and grasses. **Eggs**: 3 -6, white. **Tidbit**: The only songbird that swims.

What is my nest made of?

_____

Crater Lake

The lake is 1943 feet deep, filled by snowmelt and rain. The lake temperature varies between 32° and 66°. During the winter months, the shoreline may freeze.

At each of the pull-outs on Rim Drive, the views of The Lake are spectacular. There are so many stories to be told about the caldera. Looking at the Lake, you may see the "Old Man of the Lake," or perhaps the "Lady of the Lake." And then there is the ice cave, the grotto, the American dipper who builds its nest at the edge of melting snow along a creek. Or perhaps you can see the Wineglass, Pumice Castle, or Sun Notch, many of the geologic features of the Caldera. On the following pages a cut-out of the Lake shows you some of the many features and more stories about life below the surface of The Lake. Take at least a day and really explore the Lake. Walk down Cleetwood Trail and experience the Lake close-up. See the clarity of the water, feel how cold it is. And most of all, enjoy a beautiful sunrise or sunset at The Lake. It will truly make your day very special.

CK

Crater Lake

Instructions: Hidden in the puzzle below are some words associated with The Caldera and the Lake. Words in **bold** can be found forward, backwards, up, down, or diagonally. Circle the letters of the words as you find them in the puzzle. Write the uncircled letters on the lines below. The uncircled letters spell out how Crater Lake was formed. _____

_____

American Kestrel
Caddisfly
Common **Raven**
Cormorant
Dark-eyed Junco
Deepwater Midge
Dragonfly
Hemlocks
Horned **Lark**
Kokanee Salmon

Lodgepole Pine
Merriam Cone
Old Man of the Lake
Phantom Ship
Pine Siskin
Plankton
Thermal Vents
Water **Beetle**
Water Ouzel
White**bark** Pine
Wizard Island

Rock **Wren**
Sitka **Alder**
Spotted Sandpiper
Thermal Vents
Water **Beetle**
Water Ouzel
White**bark** Pine
Wizard Island

Phantom Ship — CK

CK
Caddisfly

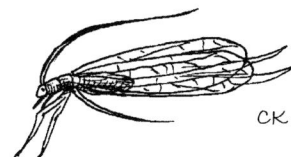
Sitka Alder
Alnus sinuata

Spotted Sandpiper
Actitus macularia
Birds often stand on one leg to conserve energy.

CK
Pumice - Volcanic rock containing many air spaces. It is very light and floats on water.

```
O K R A B E R W U D P S T D C
L L A R K E O E R I T O E ☆ O
E N D R A B E A N N D E P E R
Z C A M N N G T E O P E I N M
U D L I A O L V L W A L N O O
O P A K N N L S A E E O E C R
R R O F N A I T O F T P S M A
E K L H M A E N S E H E I A N
T Y V R R C K T A O G S I T
A L E E M C C I N H A D K R S
W H D I N O O T R M E O I R P
T L D O L U O N T E M L N E O
A G A M ☺ M ❄ ✪ Z A M M A M T
E R E D T A I L E D H A W K T
A H R A V E N O T K N A L P E
N E R W I Z A R D I S L A N D
E C I M U P Y L F S I D D A C
```

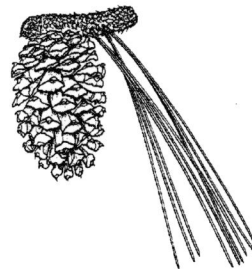
PR
Old Man of the Lake

Pine Siskin, *Corduelis pinus*

Ponderosa Pine
Pinus ponderosa

A-4

N

M

L

A-3

I

H

O

F

J

A-2

F

G

PR

Lake Legend on page 78

Lake

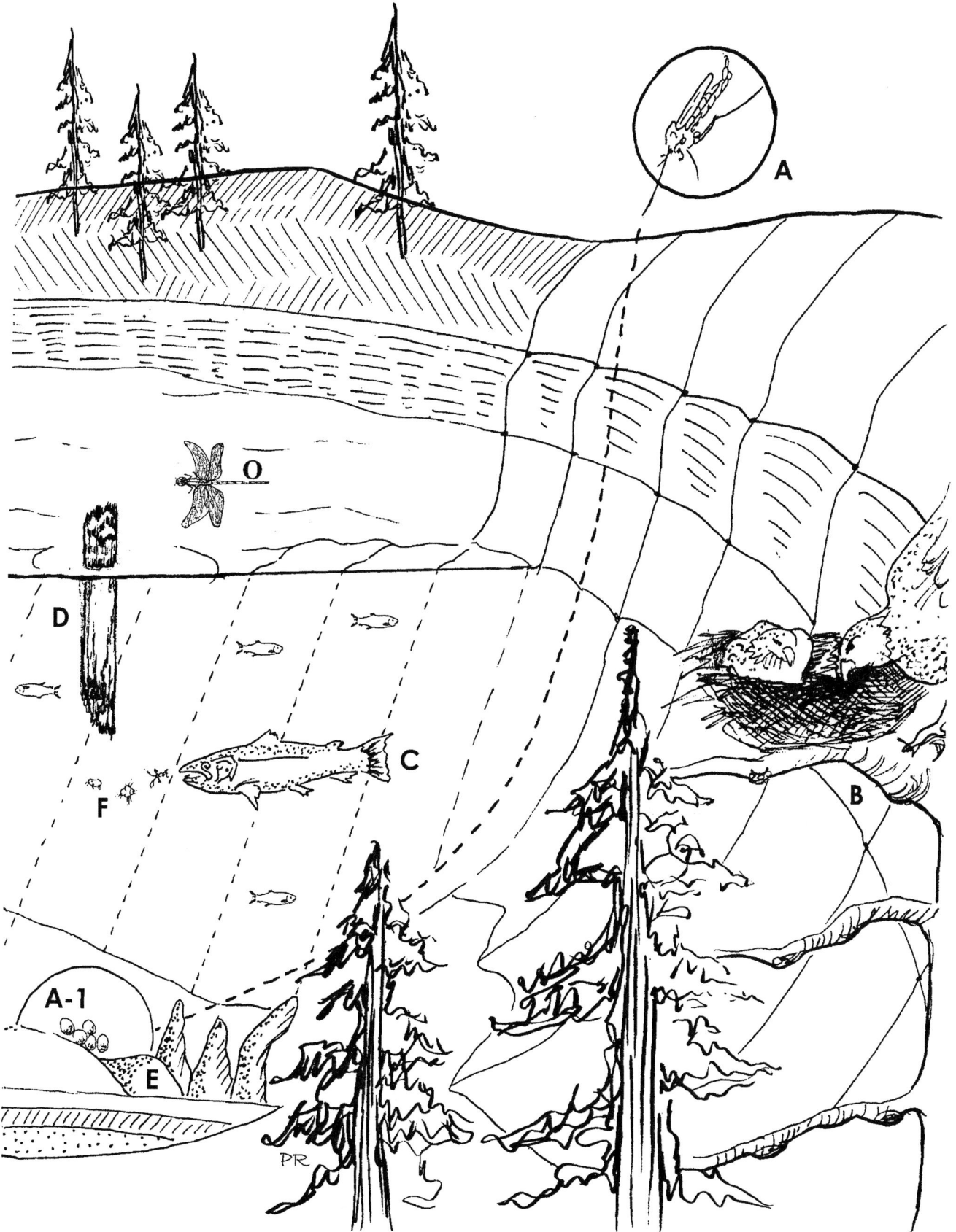

A

O

D

C

F

A-1

E

B

Inside Crater Lake

The Lake - The Color Blue

Crater Lake sits in a caldera (a Spanish word that means kettle or boiler and is used by geologists to describe a large basin-shaped volcanic depression). Over five trillion gallons of rain and snowmelt filled the lake. It holds the world record for clarity. The lake's striking cobalt blue is the result of its crystal clear water.

One of the early names for the Lake was "Deep Blue." The low concentration of nutrients in the lake results in low concentrations of plankon. This allows red, orange, yellow, and green wave lengths to penetrate deeper into the lake, while the shorter blue wave lengths scatter back to the surface and shows us a lake surface deep indigo blue.

Deep Water Midge, *Hetrotrisso cladious*

Look at the cut-out of Crater Lake on pages 76 & 77, and examine the life cycle of the of the deep water midge. As an adult it enters the water, diving to the bottom of the lake (up to 1943'), then lays its eggs (A-1). The eggs grow and hatch into larvae (A-2). They go through metamorphosis as they make their way to the surface. The larvae turn into pupa (A-3) and finally emerge from the water as an adult deep water midge (A-4)

Yellow Pollen Floating on the Lake

During the spring (June or July) parts of the lake surface may be coated yellow for a few days or weeks. Wind blows pollen from the trees on the rim and walls of the caldera and some of it lands on the lake. Eventually it sinks into the lake. Once the pollen disappears into the lake, the lake is again cobalt blue.

Hydrothermal Springs or Vents and Spires

Several thermal vents (G) exist on the floor of Crater Lake. Plankton and other microscopic organisms live around these hotspots. The hotspots are warmer than the surrounding areas of the lake floor and are rich with bacteria. The spires (E) are inactive thermal vents.

Merriam Cone

Merriam Cone, which rises approximately 486 feet above the lake floor, is the result of an eruption after the collapse of Mount Mazama. Its symmetrical shape and lack of a crater at the top indicates it was formed under water. The andesite composition is similar to the deeply submerged parts of Wizard Island volcano. The cone is near the lake's north shore.

American Dipper or Water Ouzel, *Cinclus mexicanus*

As the snowline on the caldera walls recedes, the water ouzel or the dipper builds its nest next to the receding snow. If you are standing by the Sinnott Memorial Overlook, look to your right for this bird. You may need a pair of binoculars to get a really good look at the bird and its eggs or chicks. The dipper is a common bird of creeks and streams. It is the only American songbird that swims below the surface of water and bobs cork-like after foraging on the rocky bottom.

The Lake Legion

A-	Deep Water Midge Life Cycle p. 76	**I-**	Rainbow Trout
B-	Bald Eagle Nest at Crater Lake	**J-**	Snails, Crayfish
C-	Kokanee Salmon p. 51	**K-**	Worms
D-	Old Man of the Lake p. 79	**L-**	Wizard Island p. 18
E-	Spires p. 78	**M-**	Yellow Pollen Floating on the Lake p. 78
F-	Plankton p. 51	**N-**	Llao Rock p. 14
G-	Geothermal Vents	**O-**	Aquatic Insects p. 52
H-	Merriam Cone p. 78		

The Old Man of the Lake

One of the many mysteries in the park is "The Old Man of the Lake." How old is it? Where did it come from? What kind of tree is it? How long has it been floating upright in the lake?

The first recorded observation of the "Old Man of the Lake" was in 1896 by Joseph S. Diller, United States Geological Survey geologist, who first came to the lake in 1883 on a scientfic reconnaissance. On his first trip he studied lava flows. On a later trip he built a raft and began exploring the lake.

There are many theories about the "Old Man." One theory is that before water filled Crater Lake, a forest grew on the floor of the caldera. Another suggestion is that the tree was growing on the caldera wall and when Chaski slide occurred, the tree was torn from the side of the mountain. When the caldera filled in with water, the rock laden trunk of the tree kept the tree floating upright. Today there are no rocks visible at the base of the log under water. Why it still floats upright is another mystery. Some feel that the submerged part of the log is water logged.

It has been suggested that the tree might be a western hemlock. Since DNA testing has not been performed on a sample of the tree, no one knows for sure which species of conifer it is.

The "Old Man" stands 4½' out of the water, 30' under the water, roughly 2' wide, and is perfectly balanced. Green moss grows on the log under the surface of the lake. The direction of wind determines where the Old Man travels. It has been observed directly under the Sinnott Memorial and all points north.

From July 1 to September 12, 1938, Park Naturalist Wayne E. Kartchner observed the movement of the "Old Man." In the chart below, Kartchner recorded the movement of the "Old Man" during the month of August. "It traveled 62.1 miles with a daily average of .067 mile, the maximum was 3.8 miles. During the month, the "Old Man" traveled the northern end of the lake indicating that the winds were out of the south."*

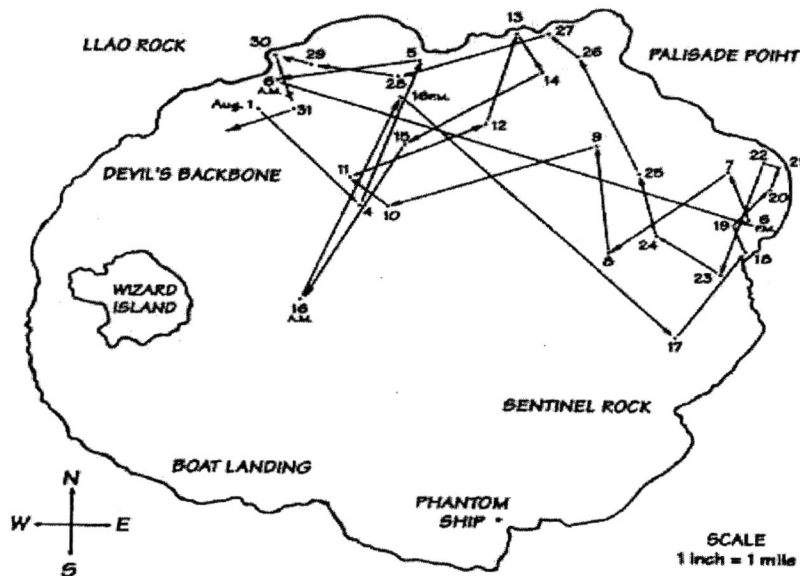

Graphic of Wind Current Route of "Old Man in the Lake" courtesy of Nature Notes, Volume XI No. 3, 1938, Crater Lake Natural History Association.

*From an article by Park Ranger Naturalist Wayne E. Kartchner, Nature Notes, Volume XI No. 3, 1938, Crater Lake Natural History Association.

Hemlock
Tsuga sp.

Mount Scott

Mount **Scott**, the highest point in the park at 8,926 feet, is 2,761 feet above the surface of the lake. This **composite** volcano is believed to have formed on the flank of Mount Mazama before it erupted. Mount Scott's very steep cone is made up of layers of **andesite** lava, which came from Mazama's magma chamber. The amphitheater (a large **cirque**) on the northwest side was eroded away by glacial action.

The peak is the perfect location to view the Klamath Basin and mountains as far south as Mount **Shasta** and Mount McLoughlin. The peak is also a great place for viewing goshawks, northern **harriers** (also called marsh hawks), red-tailed hawks, falcons, bald eagles, golden eagles, and osprey during spring and fall migration.

Whitebark pines grow at the tree line of Mount Scott. Clark's nutcrackers forage on seeds of the **whitebark pine** cone as well as food left by careless visitors at picnic areas. Other plants and animals you may see on Mount Scott are mountain hemlock, Shasta fir, Shasta knotweed, pumice **sandwort**, Anderson's lupine, rabbitbrush, goldenweed, California needlegrass, squirreltail, dwarf mountain fleabane, silvery raillardella, Lemmon's rockcress, woody stemmed rockcress, skunk-leaved **Jacob's** ladder, and **pika, marmot,** golden-mantled ground squirrel, and chipmunks.

Instructions: As you color the picture below, add some of the other plants and animals you may see on Mount Scott.

Mount Scott

Instructions: Answer the questions below and fill in the blanks in the crossword puzzle. Use the letter hints in the puzzle to help you. All of the answers are in **bold** type and are on the - Mount Scott page 80.

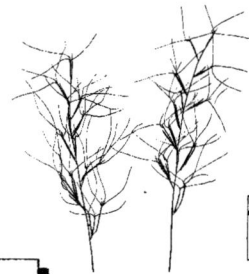

Needlegrass
Aristida oligantha

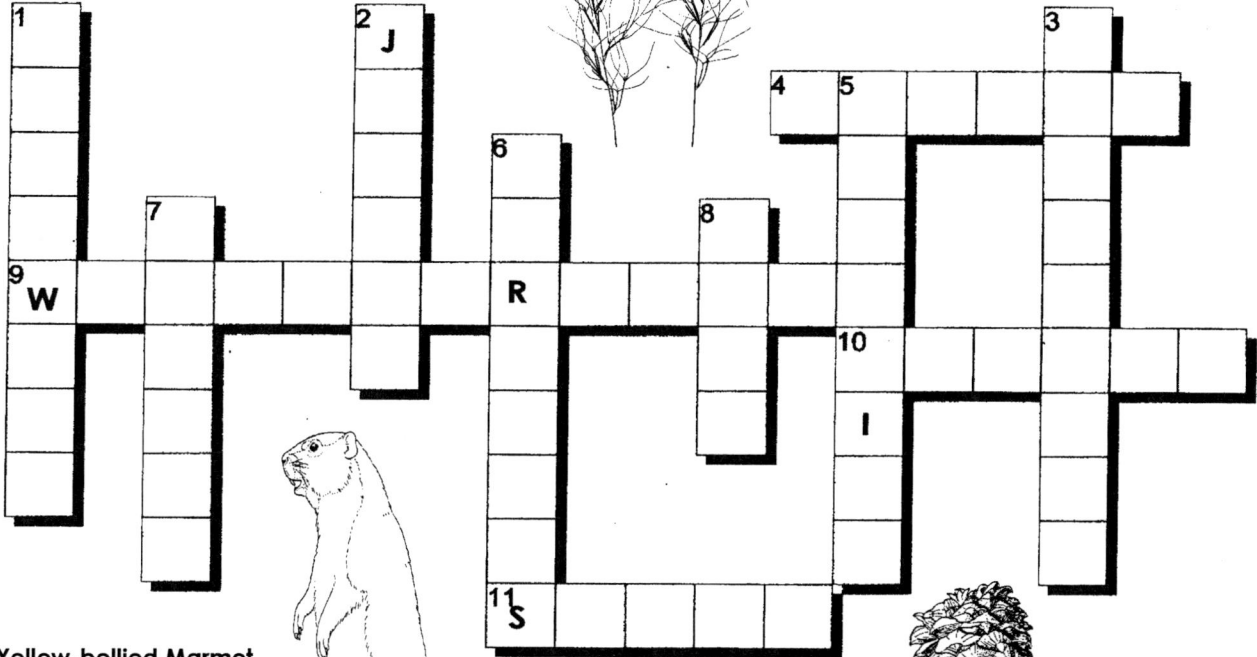

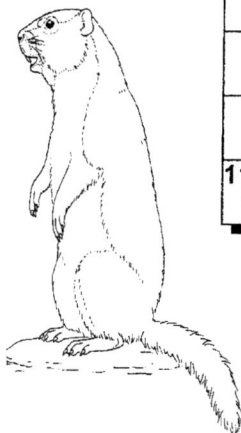

Yellow-bellied Marmot
Marmota flaviventris
Yellowish-brown with yellow belly, reddish tail with black tip.

Whitebark Pine Cone
Pinus albicaulis

Pika
Ochotona princeps
Variable color blends with the rocks. Closely related to the rabbit family.

Across

4   A small animal you may see from the trail.

9   You may see a Clark's nutcracker eating my seeds.

10 The summit of Mount Scott is a good place to see Mount S____.

11 Mount S___ was on the northern flank of Mount Mazama.

Down

1   One of the plants growing on the mountain is pumice S_____.

2   A plant you may see on the trail is skunk-leaved J_____ Ladder.

3   Mount Scott is what type of volcano?

5   Mount Scott is made up of A_____ lava.

6   During spring and fall migration you may see northern H_____.

7   Another name for the glacial amphitheater is a C_____.

8   Another small animal you may see on Mount Scott is the P_____.

Panhandle

The Panhandle section of the Park is the very accessible but uncrowded. The Panhandle is 974 acres and contains the park's greatest plant diversity (it's only rival is Red Blanket Canyon which is only partly in the park).

Because the area has so few visitors or staff visiting it, the animals are apt to ignore you. You can walk through areas of past controlled fire burns with holes in the ground that look like Bigfoot roamed the area. If you hear squirrels high up in a sugar pine tree watch a drama unfold. Perhaps a stellar jay is hovering like a helicopter below a sugar pine cone, plucking a seed. The squirrels do not want to share, so they try to chase away the jay. Perhaps a Clark's Nutcracker is also feeding on a sugar pine cone, only it perches on the cone as it stuffs itself with seeds to bury for the winter. It is also a good place to look for ruffed grouse. Look for bear scratch marks on the trees or perhaps you *hear the drilling sound* of a black-backed woodpecker searching for bark beetles in a tree nearby. Can you see the ponderosa pine tree with its puzzle-shaped bark or see a green towhee or dusky flycatcher? **Directions**: To reach the Panhandle you can park at the Ponderosa picnic area and cross the road. Walk on fire trails to spend time in this quiet and serene area.

Instructions: Part I - Color the different plants and animals you see in the picture below.
Part II - As you walk through the Panhandle, write down in your journal at the back of the book, the different plants, animals, and animal tracks you see. How many did you see?____.

Panhandle Puzzle

A variety of plants and animals live in the Panhandle section of the park. In the puzzle below are the names of the plants and animals you may see as you walk through the Panhandle.

Instructions: In the list below are some of the plants, animals, and other features found in the Panhandle. Place the words in the puzzle below. Letters of some of the words have been provided to start you out.

Bear
Black-tailed **Deer**
Black-backed **Woodpecker**
Douglas **Fir**
Forest Fire
Fox Sparrow
Gray Jay
Greenleaf Manzanita

Golden-mant led Ground Squirrel
Ponderosa Pine
Red-tailed **Hawk**
Red **Crossbill**
Root Imprint **Holes**
Ruffed **Grouse**

Stellar **Jay**
Snowbush Ceanothus
Sugar Pine
Sugar Pine **Cone**
Sugar Pine Cone **Seed**
Yellow-rumped Warbler

The hole (a tree well) is all that is left of what was once a tree burned in a fire.

Golden-mantled Ground Squirrel

Black Bears

A **sugar pine cone** that was stripped of its seeds by a bear.

Stellar jay hovering while plucking a seed from a sugar pine or white pine cone

Black-tailed Deer

-83-

Pumice Desert and Pumice Fields

The Pumice Desert and the pumice fields are miles of fragile and inhospitable land and poor soil. Deposits of pumice in these areas may be up to 200' deep.

The Pumice Desert and pumice fields around the park are called successional areas because the ecosystem was destroyed by the eruption of Mount Mazama. Regrowth after a forest fire, for example, begins the next year with many wildflowers blooming and whitebark pine and lodgepole pine seedlings sprouting in the nutrient rich soils (see Forest Fires on page 96). In the Pumice Desert and pumice fields, regrowth takes much longer due to extreme temperatures, a lack of moisture and nutrients. Water collects in the pores of the pumice or deep into the soil, leaving little moisture at the surface. Organic materials brought by wind, water, birds, and animals may take hundreds of years to build up. Slowly, these areas are returning to life. The eruption pulverized the "soil" so much that it still tests >90% sterile.

Lodgepole pine has adapted to this harsh environment. As you travel throughout the park notice the open areas surrounded by forests of lodgepole pine as well as seedlings and trees of various sizes sprinkled throughout the desert and fields.

Pumice Desert and Pumice Fields

Plants that have adapted to the harsh environment of the Pumice Desert include whitebark pine, subalpine **fir**, mountain **hemlock**, pumice **moonwort**, pumice **sandwort**, Oregon **sedge**, Newberry fleeceflower, **yellow** staining collomia, prairie lupine, mountain **buckwheat**, Mount Shasta sedge, pine **violet**, **pussypaws**, and mountain buckwheat. Some of the animals, or their tracks, you may see at the Pumice Desert are **coyote**, Mazama pocket **gopher**, deer **mouse**, bushy-tailed **woodrat**, **chipmunk**, porcupine, snowshoe **hare**, mule **deer**, **elk**, red fox, **ermine** (short-tailed weasel), long-tailed **weasel**, big brown **bats**, horned **lark**, mountain **bluebird**, Cassin's **finch**, dark-eyed junco, and chipping sparrow.

Instructions: **Part I** - Sit quietly in the Pumice Desert and listen for bird calls, wind rustling in the trees. You may record your observations in the journal at the back of the book. Color the illustration of the Pumice Desert. If you see any animals or insects, draw them in the picture. How many different species of plants and animals did you see while you were at the Pumice Desert and at various pumice fields around the Park?_____ **Part II -** In the description of the Pumice Desert and pumice fields are words in **bold** type. Place those words in the puzzle below. Letters of several words have been provided to start you out.

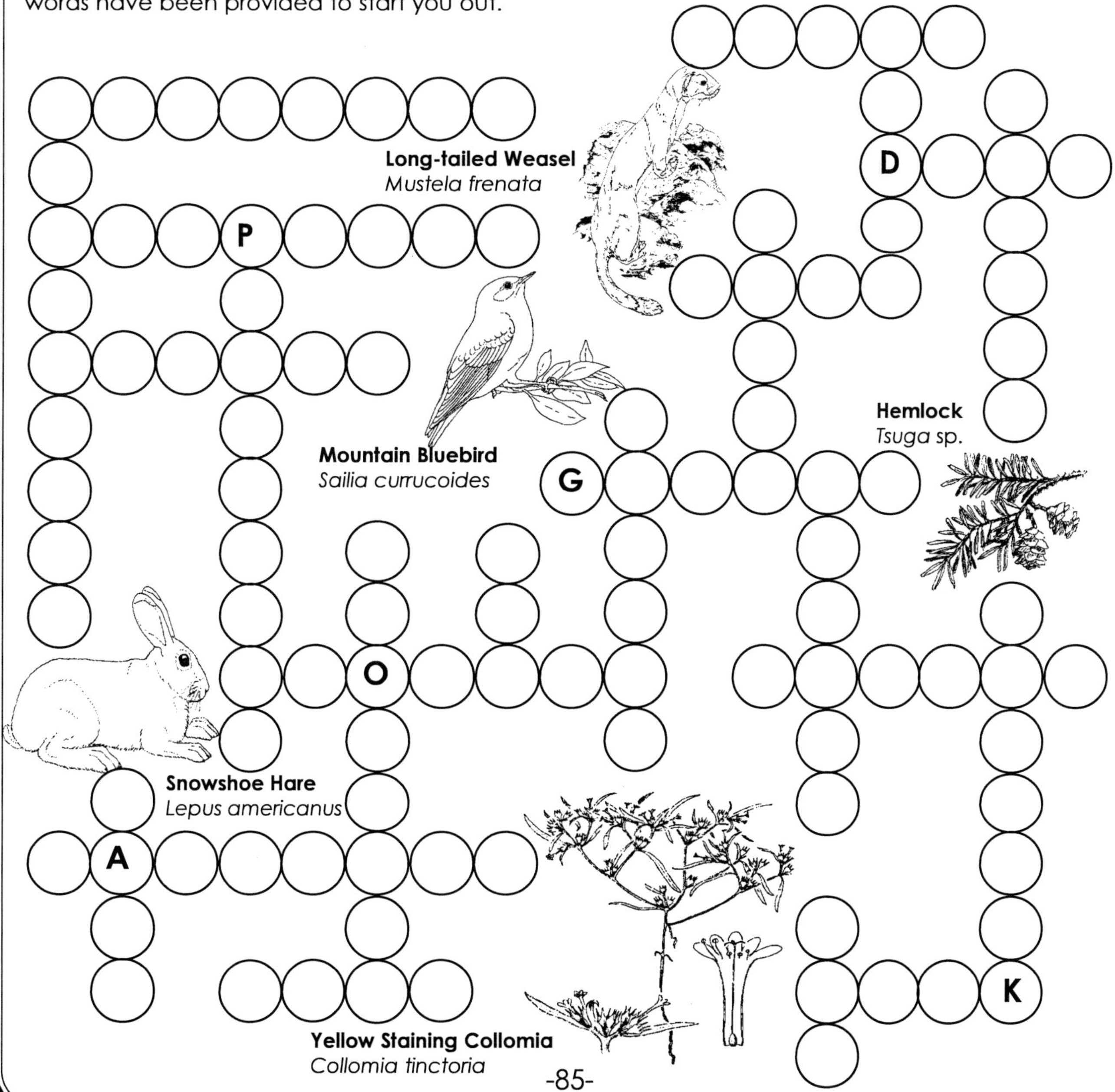

Long-tailed Weasel
Mustela frenata

D

P

Mountain Bluebird
Sailia currucoides

G

Hemlock
Tsuga sp.

O

Snowshoe Hare
Lepus americanus

A

K

Yellow Staining Collomia
Collomia tinctoria

Sphagnum Bog

Sphagnum Bog is one of four Research Natural Areas of the Park. Scientists visit the park and study its plant life and water quality. A bog, or mire as it is technically known, is characterized by peat, acid, and standing water which comes from rain and snowmelt. Sometimes the sphagnum moss mingles with aquatic plants and forms a mossy mat and the entire bog becomes carpeted. The sphagnum moss may become substrate for other aquatic plants.

Many of the plants that live in bogs are specially adapted to high acidity, low oxygen and a soggy substrate. Bladderworts and sundew get their food in a very unusual way - they trap and digest insects and other tiny animals. You may also see dragonflies and tadpoles; blue and other butterflies flit from flower to flower; deer, elk, bear, pine marten, and other large mammals visit bogs at various times of the year to find food, water, and shelter. Some of the plants you may see at the Bog are round-leaved sundew, long-leaved sundew, sphagnum moss, mountain bladderwort, horsetail, and fireweed.

Instructions: Draw in a pool of standing water. Add some tadpoles, butterflies, dragonflies, pine marten, or other animals you might see there.

CK

Sphagnum Bog Plants

Plant Checklist

Trees

Englemann Spruce *Picea engelmannii*
Lodgepole Pine *Pinus contorra murrayana*
Subalpine Fir *Abies lasiocarpa*

Shrubs

Littleleaf Huckleberry *Vaccinium scoparium*
Mountain Alder *Alnus incana*
Swamp Gooseberry *Ribes lacustre*
Western Blueberry *Vaccinium uliginosum*

Herbs

Alpine Pyrola *Pyrola asarifolia*
Alpine Shootingstar *Dodecatheon alpinum*
Alpine Wintergreen *Gaultheria humifusa*
American Bistort *Polygonum bistorides*
Arrowleaf Groundsel *Senecio triangularis*
Bog St. Johnswort *Hypericum anagalloides*
Camas *Camassia leichtinii suksdorfii*
Campanula *Collomia mazama*
Common Bladderwort *Utricularia vulgaris*
Elephant's Head *Pedicularis groenlandica*
False Hellebore *Veratrum viride*
Fireweed *Epilobium augustifolium*

Horsetail *Equisetum arvense*
Ladie's Tresses *Spiranthes romanzoffiana*
Leathery Grape Fern *Botrychium multifidum*
Long-leaved Sundew *Drosera anglica*
Marsh Marigold *Caltha biflora*
Monkshood *Acontium columbianum*
Musk Flower *Mimulus moschatus moschatus*
One-flowered Gentian *Gentiana simplex*
Pond Lily *Nuphar polysepalum*
Primrose Monkeyflower *Mimulus primuloides*
Queen's Cup *Clintonia uniflora*
Rosy Twited Stalk *Streptopus roseus*
Round-leaved Sundew *Drosera rotundifolia*
Scarlet Paintbrush *Castelleja miniata*
Sphagnum Moss *Sphagnum squarrosum*
Slender Bog Orchid *Platanthera stricta*
Stream Violet *Viola glabella*
Swamp Whitehead
    Spehnosciadium capitellatum
Swamp Willowherb *Epilobium palustre*
Tall Bluebell *Mertensia paniculata*
Tofieldia *Tofieldia glutinosa brevistyla*
Twin-flower *Linnae borealis*
Veronica *Veronica americana*
White Bog Orchid *Platanthera leucostachys*
Willow Herb *Epilobium glandulosum*

Yellow Monkeyflower *Mimulus guttatus*

Cross section of a bog. In the Sphagnum Bog area of the park, there are two or three areas of standing water. Depending upon the time of year, you may have to walk through soggy soils. Englemann spruce, lodgepole pine, and subalpine fir surround the bog. During June many of the shrubs and herbs listed on the checklist bloom at the bog. As with Castle Crest Wildflower Trail and other areas within the park, spring comes late, during June, July, and August. Pools of standing water are higher during the early summer months, due to rain and snow melt. If you visit the bog in June you may see tadpoles swimming in the pools. **Please be careful and help us protect the bog by not stepping on plants or disturbing wildlife.**

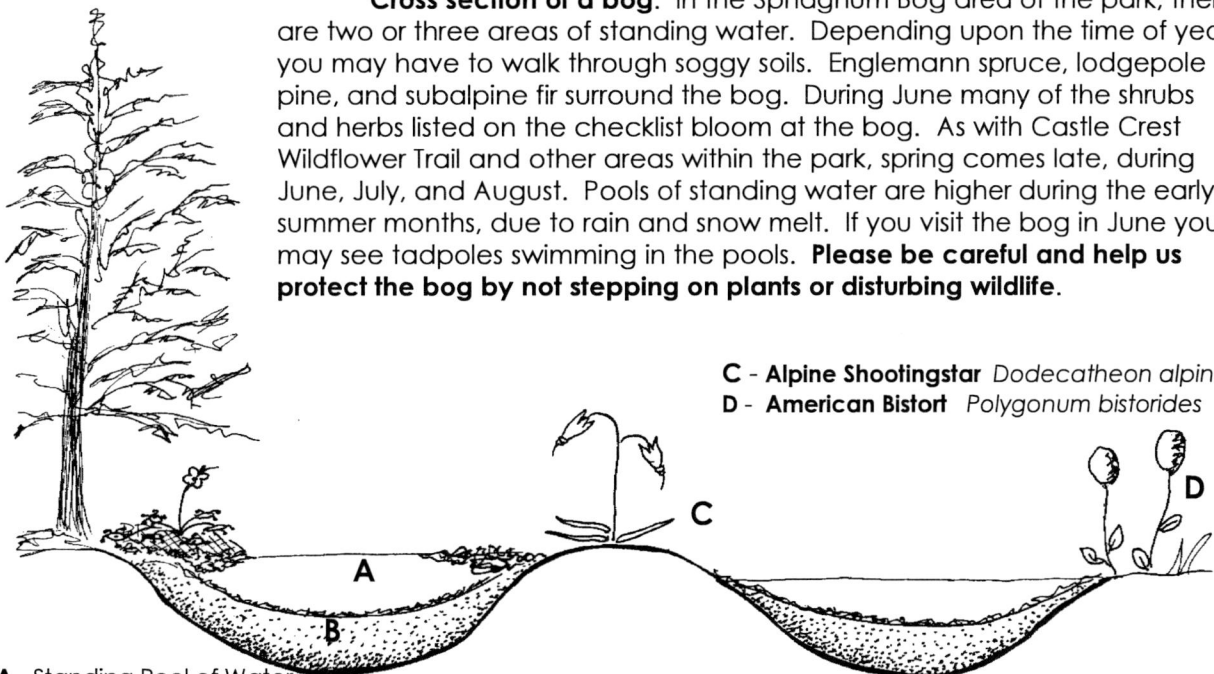

C - Alpine Shootingstar *Dodecatheon alpinum*
D - American Bistort *Polygonum bistorides*

A - Standing Pool of Water
B - Layer of Peat

Plants of Sphagnum Bog

Instructions: **Part I** - Draw a line between the plant and its name. **Hint**: If you need help in identifying the plant, check the *Sphagnum Bog Plant Checklist* on page 87. On the list are both the common name of the plant as well as its scientific name. **Part II** - Color the plants.

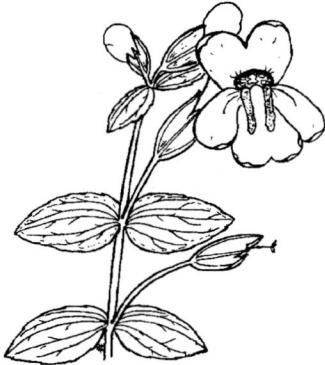

Marsh Marigold

Tall Bluebell

Scarlet Paintbrush

Common Bladderwort

Horsetail

Round-leaved Sundew

Yellow Monkeyflower

Mimulus guttatus
Flowers: Yellow with small, crimson spots on lower lip.
Leaves: Green.

Mertensia paniculata
Flowers: Blue, sometimes pink.
Leaves: Green.

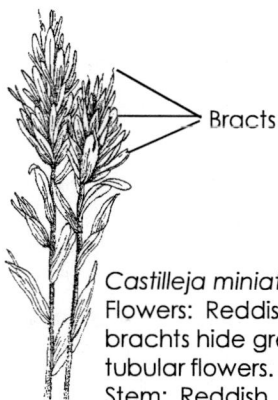

Bracts

Castilleja miniata
Flowers: Reddish brachts hide green tubular flowers.
Stem: Reddish Brown.
Leaves: Green

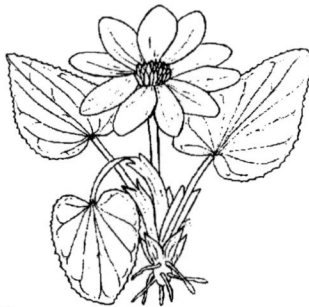

Caltha biflora
Flowers: White with yellow centers. Leaves: Green

—Chris Ely

Drosera rotundifolia
Flowers: White.
Leaves: Green with long, reddish hairs.

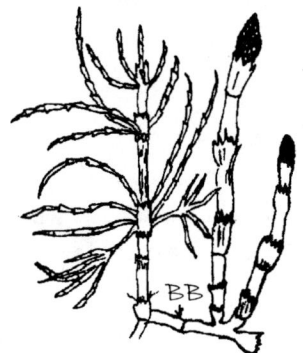

BB

Equisetum arvense
Plant: Green.

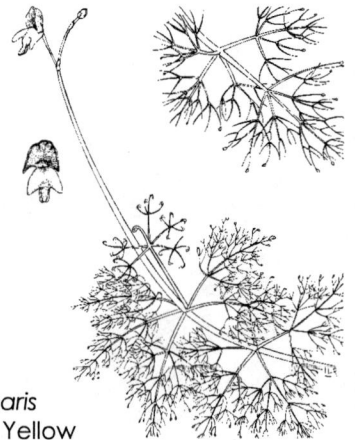

Utricularia vulgaris
Flowers: Deep Yellow
Leaves: Mossy Green

Sphagnum Bog Crossword Puzzle

Instructions: Answer the questions below and fill in the blanks in the crossword puzzle. Answers can be found on the Sphagnum Bog pages 86 - 88.

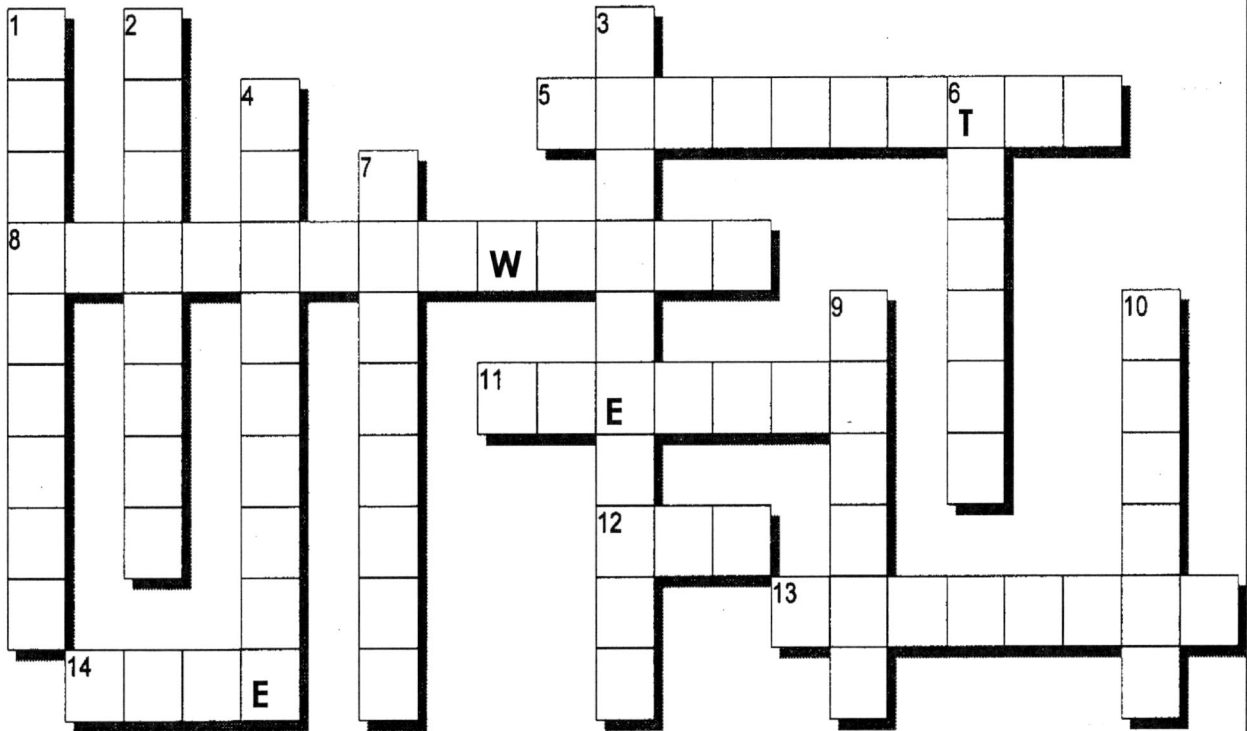

Sphagnum Moss

Across

5)   A P___M_____ may be seen scampering on the boulders along the bog trail.
8)   One of the characteristics of a bog is S_____W____.
11)   Animals find food, water, and S_____ at the bog.
12)   At dawn you may see E__ at one of the pools.
13)   Along the trail you may see large holes drilled in a tree by a P_____ woodpecker.
14)   I am a B___ butterfly.

DOWN

1)   I have silica in my stalk and branches. I am a H_____.
2)   The bog gets its name from S_____ moss.
3)   One of the shrubs you may see is a L_____ huckleberry.
4)   Around the edge of the bog you can see a forest of L_____ pine.
6)   Occasionally you may see a red-headed, bald T_____ vulture flying overhead.
7)   My water comes from rain and S_____.
9)   I am a white bog O_____.
10)   I am an insect eating plant. My name is round-leaved S_____.

Turkey Vulture
Gathartes aura

Pileated Woodpecker,
Dryocopus pileatus

American (Pine) Marten,
Martes americana

Whitebark Pine seedling at U.S. Forest Service Nursery.

Deep submersible. Illustration courtesy of the National Park Service.

Resource Management Projects

The 1916 Organic Act mandated the creation of the National Park Service. The Act also mandated the National Park Service to protect and preserve parks and conserve their natural resources for future generations. At Crater Lake National Park, land managers are revegetatiug disturbed areas with native plants, monitoring ecosystems for changes, using geographic information systems to store information about the park's terrestrial and aquatic resources. On the following pages are several projects the park is actively involved in. At the Science and Learning Center, which opened in August 2006, scientists and students come from all over the United States to study park resources and help gather invaluable information to protect the natural resources of Crater Lake National Park and the area and other ecosystems. Lake water quality and clarity are constantly being monitored (see page 91). Another study currently underway is a study of deepwater moss growing at 100 to 400 feet under the surface of Crater Lake. In 1988, park aquatic biologist Mark Buktenica, riding in a submersible, was able to chart the bottom of Crater Lake and collect samples of benthic flora and fauna.

Lake Management

The Aquatic Ecologist at Crater Lake National Park is responsible for monitoring the health of the Lake and creeks, and the plants and animals that live there. Some of the tools the ecologist and biologists use are illustrated below.

A Secchi disk is used to determine water clarity of Crater Lake. It is an eight inch metal disk painted black and white. It is lowered into the water until no longer visible. Water clarity in the Lake has been registered at 142'. Although the lake is the 7th deepest in the world, it holds the world record for clarity.

The Deep Rover is a one-person submersible used in studying hydrothermal vents, plants, and animals living at bottom of the Lake. These studies will help monitor changes to the Lake and the information will be studied by managers of other lakes around the world. Deep Rover also surveyed the bottom in 1988, and eventually helped produced a map of the bottom.

The deepest point of the lake is indicated by a buoy. This buoy contains a variety of weather equipment for measuring water temperature, air temperature, humidity, and wind speed.

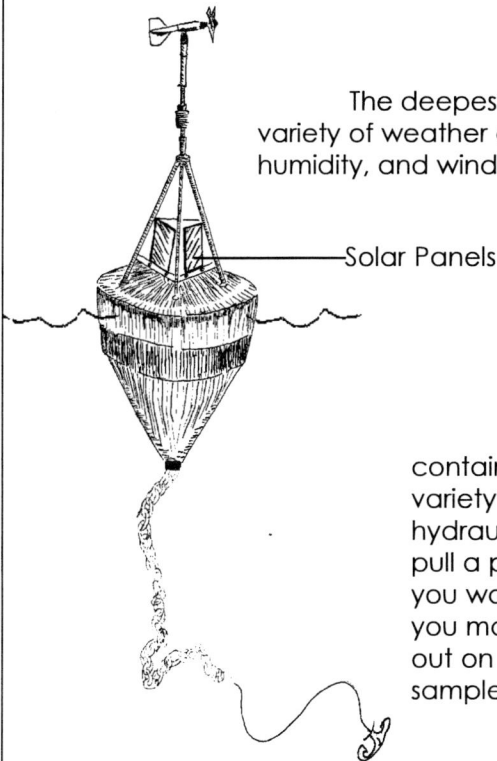

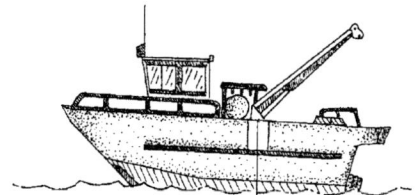

Solar Panels

Crater Lake has a research vessel which contains all of the latest equipment to conduct a variety of tests. R/V Neuston is equipped with a hydraulic system which can lower the secchi disk, pull a plankton net, and perform other taskss. If you walk down to the dock at Cleetwood Cove, you may see it moored there or you may see it out on the Lake conducting tests, or collecting samples for research projects.

Illustrations of the Deep Rover courtesy of the National Park Service. Illustrations of the buoy, research vessel R/V Neuston, and the Secchi Disk by PR.

Bull Trout and Sun Creek Restoration Project
Bull Trout vs Brook Trout

Between 1929 and 1971 over 200,000 brook trout were **introduced** to **Sun Creek** so there would be more fish available for **fishermen**. The brook trout, an introduced (non-native species) is more agressive in seeking both food and the best habitat along the creek. There was some cross-breeding of the two species. As a result, the numbers of the **native** species - bull trout - began to decline. In 1989, a survey showed there were less than 130 adult fish in the creek and only in a 1.2 mile stretch of the creek. **Resource** Management staff of biologists, through their mandate to protect and **conserve** the natural resources of the park, put together the Bull Trout Restoration Project. The goal was to re-establish the native bull trout within the Park boundary, remove brook trout, and place a **barrier** so that the brook **trout** could not return to the park.

In 1992, the restoration project began. Using nets, some of the brook trout were removed from the park. A rock and log barrier on Sun Creek was constructed near the park boundary to prevent the re-introduction of non-native book trout.

In 2001, 243 mature bull trout were observed, as well as many **fry** along the creek shoreline and around **gravel** beds. By 2001, they occupied more than seven miles*. Sightings increased from a 1.2 mile stretch of Sun Creek in 1989 to more than seven miles in 2001.*

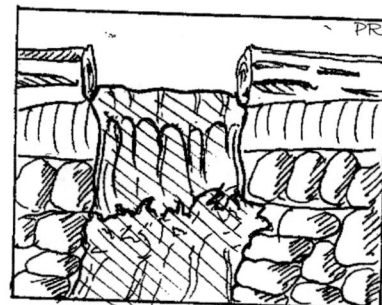

A rock and log barrier on Sun Creek

Information provided by Mark Buktenica, Crater Lake Aquatic Ecologist in interviews & from his article on bull trout in Crater Lake Nature Notes (1992).

Bull Trout, *Salvelinus confluentus*
Native species in Sun Creek. <u>Weight</u>: 4 to 20 lbs. Small pale **yellow** to **crimson** spots on olive-green to brown above, fading to white on belly. Spawning adults develop red on belly. <u>Habitat</u>: Creeks, rivers, and lakes. **<u>Diet</u>:** Young eat insects, adults eat other fish. **<u>Spawn</u>**: Fall, after water temperatures drop below 48°F. <u>Eggs</u>: Eggs require four to five months incubation period.

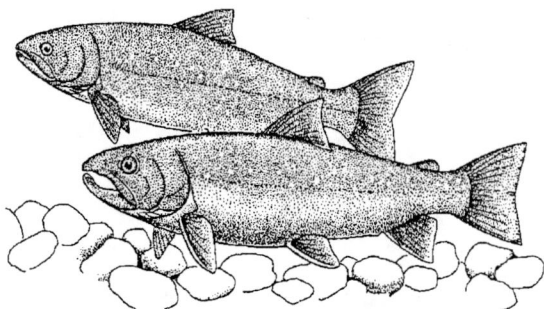

When do I spawn?

Brook Trout *Salvelinus fontinalis*
Non-native species. <u>Length</u>: 8 to 21". Olive green above with dark wavy lines, sides olive, with many large yellowish spots and few small red spots with blue halos. **Belly** white, reddish in adult male. Dorsal fin spotted, triangular; tail fin squared or lightly forked; ventral fins reddish, with white and black leading edge. Large jaw extends well behind eyes. <u>Habitat</u>: Lakes, cool clear **headwater** ponds, spring-fed streams in mountains. Cascade Mountain Range in Washington & Oregon. <u>Diet:</u> Young eat insects, adults eat insects and other fish.

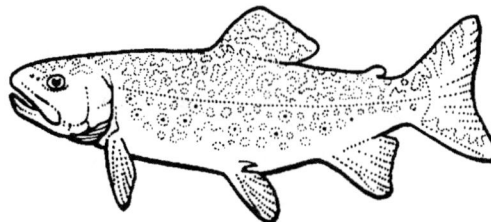

What do I eat?

Illustration of Bull Trout courtesty of USFWS.

Bull Trout and Sun Creek Restoration Project
Bull Trout vs Brook Trout
Puzzle

Instructions: In the descriptions on the previous page, some words are in **bold** type face. Place those words in the puzzle below. The first letter of several of the words has been provided to start you out.

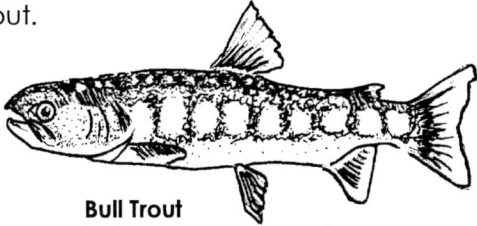

Bull Trout
Salvelinus confluentu

Diet of a trout eggs, larvae, and nympths.

Life Stages of a Trout

A - Egg - laid and develops in gravel.

B - Fry - tiny fry swim out of the gravel and begin to eat insects and other food.

C - Smolt - they swim lower in the creek.

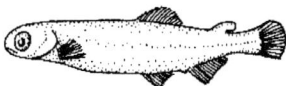

D - Adult - Although they do not migrate to the ocean, they do return to the same gravel spot to spawn their eggs.

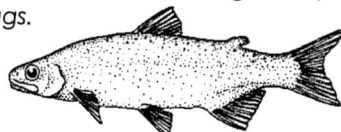

Whitebark Pine Blister Rust Research Project

"Whitebark pine is a keystone species at Crater Lake National Park. Nearly half of the Park's west-side trees are dead or dying from blister rust, a non-native fungal disease imported from northern Asia. The Park's long-term goal is to retain whitebark pine by ensuring native disease-resistant seedlings are regenerating. However, initial testing of resistance and restoration techniques is required to guide our efforts. We intend to: 1) test disease-resistance and cone collection techniques for at least 25 parent trees; 2) survey stands and implement an appropriate planting strategy for rust-resistant progeny, and 3) mark and map plantings for monitoring. Immediate results will provide critical guidance for our planned conservation efforts. Collection and dissemination results will be applicable to other Parks which have whitebark pine."*

The Project

At each of the 25 selected trees, the terrestrial ecologist and his staff place wire mesh cages over 10 immature blister-rust-free whitebark pine cones at the top of each tree. The few cages allow the Clark's nutcracker to harvest most of the seeds but saves some for research and replanting the whitebark pine forest. In the fall, the Terrestrial Ecologist uncages the mature blister-rust-free whitebark pine cones and picks the seeds out of the cones. Whitebark pine seeds are taken to a Forest Service nursery where the seeds are planted. The whitebark pine seedlings will be infected with the blister rust fungus to see if they remain restitant to the fungus. If they are resistant, more cones on the resistant trees will be caged in the park and more seeds planted at the nursery.

When it is determined that the seedlings are blister rust resistant, the whitebark pine seedlings will be planted in the park to replace those that are dead and dying as a result of the blister rust fungus. The goal of the Blister Rust Fungus project is to plant new forests of whitebark pines to be visited by the Clark's nutcracker. Each nutcracker bury 20,000 to 30,000 whitebark pine seeds each year. Future generations will be able to see how Crater Lake National Park has preserved and conserved the whitebark pine tree.

Instructions: Walk to the rim and look at a whitebark pine tree or drive to a stand of whitebark pines along rim drive. Do you see a Clark's nutcracker or golden-mantled ground squirrel near the tree? Perhaps a deer is browsing on grass nearby. In the journal at the back of this book, write what you think it would be like if all the white-bark pine trees were gone.

Blister rust starts at the top of the tree and spreads to the lower part of the tree, killing it. The Crater Lake Currant is host to the blister rust fungi and it spreads from the currant to the whitebark pine tree. Photograph of blister rust by Dr. Michael Murray.

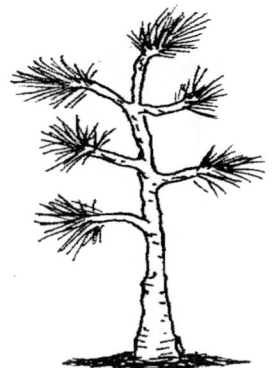

The abstract from "Determining Disease-resistance and Restoration Techniques for Declining Whitebark Pine Populations" by Michael Murray, Ph.D., Crater Lake Terrestrial Ecologist, and Edward G. Schreiner, United States Geological Survey, Forest and Rangeland Ecosystem Science Center.

Whitebark Pine Blister Rust Research Project

Instructions: Illustrated below are steps of the Blister Rust Research Project. Write the # of the activity on the line near the picture that best describes the restoration activity that Resource Managers are taking to help restore whitebark pine forests to Crater Lake National Park.

5 - Orchard ladder

6 - Placing wire mesh cages over immature blister- rust-free white bark pine cones.

3 - Wire mesh cages

2 - Whitebark pine cone seeds are taken to a Forest Service nursery where the seeds are planted.

1 - The goal of the Blister Rust Fungus project is to plant new forests of disease resistant whitebark pines.

4 - Mature blister-rust- free whitebark pine cones are picked.

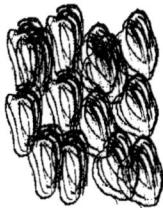

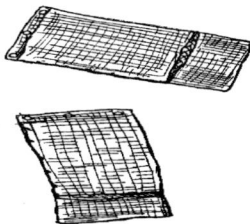

5

All illustrations this page by CK.

Forest Fires

Forest fires are common in places that experience extended periods of dry and hot weather during summer and fall, and during times of drought. When fallen branches, leaves, pine needles, moss, and other materials on the forest floor dry out they become highly flammable.

Many wildfires are started by lightning strikes. Others are caused by not thoroughly putting out a campfire or the careless toss of a burning cigarette. Today, lightning fires are accepted as a natural part of forest ecosystems. In the past wildfires were suppressed and fire fuels were allowed to build up. One measure in preventing major wildfire disasters is through **controlled burns**, which reduce the underbrush and other fuels. Then when a lightning strike occurs, the fire may scar trees and burn the understory but usually less damage is done to the forest and the wildlife living there.

Succession of Life

Immediately after a wildfire, life begins returns to the forest. Many seeds and rhizones, root crowns are still there, just hidden under the ground. Nutrients from the burned material enrich the soil and encourage new growth. Fire can thin the forest, including vegetation, the thick canopy of leaves, that prevent sunlight from reaching new growth on the forest floor. The first plants to appear are wildflowers, grasses, and shrubs. For animals that eat plants, the renewal after a forest fire means a plentiful supply of nutritious food. Deer and elk return to a habitat with many new sources of food.

Controlled Burns at Crater Lake

The "Panhandle" section of the park is a good place to see evidence of controlled burns. Many trees have burn scars but are still living. Roots of live trees do not burn during a forest fire. The tree wells you see show where a dead tree was. The dead tree stumps burn out and leave a large hole in the ground.

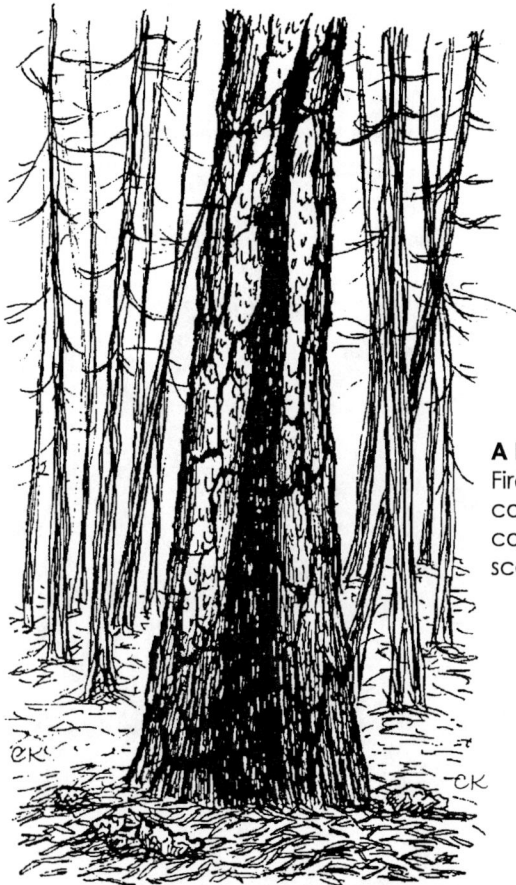

Burned Root - All that is left of a dead tree after a controlled burn , which opens up the tree canopy, allowing light in and other trees to grow.

A Fire Scar in the Panhandle - Fire touched this tree during a controlled burn. The tree continues to grow around the fire scar.

Hole - The tree and its roots are gone. There are many of these holes in the Panhandle section of the park.

Forest Fires

"Fire has been a very important natural process at Desert Creek, one of the Research Natural areas of the park. Lightning-caused fires were once as common as every nine years. These were primarily underburns which thinned the understory shrubs and allowed young pines to establish. Because fires were suppressed for most of the 1900s, the Park began to carefully introduce fire with prescribed burns in the 1970s. Monitoring plots are measured by Fire Effects Monitoring Teams."*

In late fall and early spring months, some park and forest rangers may start prescribed or controlled burns to protect our forests and the wildlife that use the forest for food and shelter.

Backfires

In addition to machinery and hand tools, firefighters may stop a forest fire by starting backfires. A backfire is a small fire that is set directly in the path of a large fire. It burns away from an established fireline toward the advancing wildfire and consumes the brush and vegetation in the larger fire's path, depriving the wildfire of its fuel. With backfires, firefighters literally fight fire with fire.

A backfire being lit by a firefighter.

Controlled Burns

Controlled or prescribed burns, help prevent a buildup of forest litter and keep the forest healthy. These fires burn quickly.

Before setting a fire, firefighters study the weather. If conditions are right, a fire line is constructed around the entire area to be burned. Then a carefully controlled fire is set inside the fire line.

Controlled burns reduce the buildup of fuels, improve habitat for wildlife, help foresters control insects, and return nutrients to the soil.

by Michael Murray, Ph.D., National Park Service Terrestrial Ecologist, from his article on the Research Natural Areas of Crater Lake National Park.

A controlled or prescribed burn prevents a buildup of fuel.

A Fire Fighter and Gear

Instructions: Below is a picture of a firefighter and his fire gear. Unscramble the name of the gear and write it on the line below the name. Circle the gear on the firefighter and draw a line between the name of the gear and firefighter and his gear.

N I T E Y D A M

_____

SVELGO

_____

OTOBS

_____

WASHAINC

_____

EAX

AXE
_____

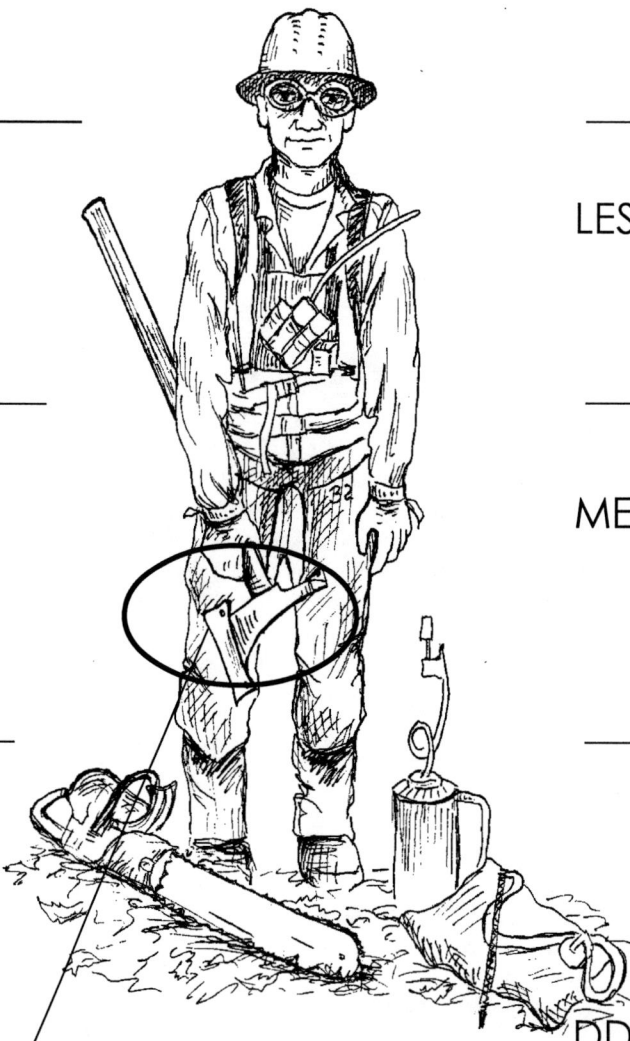

PRDI HCTOR

_____

LESGOGG

_____

METHEL

_____

DDERALB AGB

_____

E RFI TNADTARRE MROFINU

_____

Junior Ranger Program

Explore the Park and learn about the plants, animals, geology, and history of Crater Lake National Park. Through a series of activities and attendance at ranger-led programs, the visitors ages 6 - 12 years old may earn a Junior Ranger Badge. In addition to learning about the park, the young people learn about the mission of the National Park Service and become stewards of the environment. After the children receive their Junior Ranger Badge, they can share their experience with family and friends and tell them how important it is to preserve our National Park lands and our communities.

When visiting the park, you can pick up a Junior Ranger Booklet at the Steele Visitor Center. The Junior Ranger program meets at Mazama Campground amphitheater (between D & E loops at 5:00 p.m. daily) and lasts one hour.

Upon completion of the Junior Ranger program, the visitor receives a Junior Ranger badge.

Ranger Tom shows a ponderosa pine cone to a participant in the Junior Ranger Program.

Lodgepole Pine *Pinus contorta.* The tree grows 30 to 80' tall. The size of the cone varies from 1 to 1 3/4" long. Needles are bluish green in bundles of 2, 1 to 2½" long.

Sugar Pine *Pinus lambertiana.* The tree grows to 70 to 150' tall. The size of the cone varies from 11 to 20" long. Needles are bluish green in bundles of 5, 2 to 3 ½" long.

Journaling

Journals are a great place for recording your thoughts, feelings, and observations about the things you observe during your visit to Crater Lake National Park. Whether you write about or draw your visit - the smell of the bark of a tree, the sounds of wind blowing through the leaves - these memories will come alive each time you look back at your journal. Short sentences or even a simple word can be used in creating a poem or an essay on "what I saw at Crater Lake."

In addition to writing or drawing, you may make a rubbing of a leaf or trace a deer track. Be creative and have fun. To start your nature journal, go back to your favorite place at the Park, sit or lie down and get comfortable, describe your surroundings in as much detail as possible, and write about how you feel being here right now.

Bibliography

Beverley, Claire & David Ponsonby. 2003. *The Anatomy of Insects & Spiders*. San Francisco: Chronicle Books.

Cranson, K.R. 2005. *Crater Lake: Gem of the Cascades*. Lansing, MI: KRC Press.

Crater Lake Natural History Association. 1928 - 2001. *Nature Notes from Crater Lake*. Crater Lake, Oregon. See www.nps.gov/crla

Eder, Tamara. 2002. *Mammals of Washington and Oregon.* Renton, WA: Lone Pine Printing.

Follett, Dick. 1979. *Birds of Crater Lake National Park.* Crater Lake, Oregon: Crater Lake Natural History Association. Out of print.

Harmon, Rich. 2002. *Crater Lake National Park: A History*: Corvallis: Oregon State University Press.

Harrington, H.D. and L.W. Durrell. 1957. *HOW TO IDENTIFY PLANTS.* Athens, Ohio: Swallow Press.

Harris, Ann and Esther Tuttle. 1972. *Geology of National Parks*. Dubuque, Iowa: Kendal/Hunt Publishing Company.

Hill, Richard L. 2004. *Volcanoes of the Cascades, Their Rise and Their Risks*. Guilford, Connecticut. The Globe Pequot Press.

Knobel, Edward. 1980. *Field Guide to the Grasses, Sedges and Rushes of the United States*. New York: Dover Publications, Inc.

Lanner, Ronald M. 1996. *Made for Each Other: A Symbiosis of Birds and Pines*. New York: Oxford University Press.

Lapham, Stanton C. 1931. *The Enchanted Lake, Mount Mazama and Crater Lake in Story, History and Legend*. Portland Oregon: The J. K. Gill Company.

McMinn, Howard & Evelyn Maino. 1963. *Pacific Coast Trees*. Berkeley, California: University of California Press.

Pojar, Jim and Andy MacKinnon. 2004. *Plants of the Pacific Northwest Coast: Washington, Oregon, British Columbia & Alaska.* Auburn, Washington: Lone Pine Publishing.

Ross, Charles R. 1983. *Ferns to Know in Oregon*. Corvallis, Oregon.

Sharpe, Grant and Wenonah. 1959. *101 Wildflowers of Crater Lake National Park.* Seattle, Washington: University of Washington Press.

Shaw Historical Library. 2001. *The MOUNTAIN with a hole in the top - REFLECTIONS ON CRATER LAKE.* Klamath Falls, Oregon: Oregon Institute of Technology, Oregon.

Sheldon, Ian. 1997. *Animal Tracks of Washington and Oregon*. Auburn, Washington: Lone Pine Publishing.

Thomas, April Azary. 2003. *Discovering Lithia Park*. Ashland, Oregon: Adventures in Nature.

Thomas, April Azary. 2005. *Discovering North Mountain Park*. Ashland, Oregon: Ashland Parks & Recreation Division, City of Ashland.

Toops, Constance M. 1990. *Crater Lake National Park Trails*. Crater Lake, Oregon: Crater Lake Natural History Association.

Turner, Mark & Phyllis Gustafson. 2006. *Wildflowers of the Pacific Northwest*. Portland, Oregon: Timber Press, Inc.

Warfield, Ron. 1997. *A Guide to Crater Lake - The Mountain That Used to Be*. Crater Lake, Oregon: Crater Lake Natural History Association.

Yocom, Charles F. 1964. *Shrubs of Crater Lake National Park*. Crater Lake, Oregon: Crater Lake Natural History Association.

Zika, Peter F. 2003. *A Crater Lake National Park Vascular Plant Checklist*. Crater Lake, Oregon: Crater Lake Natural History Association.

Field Guides - *Birds, Mammals, Butterflies, Wildflowers, Reptiles & Amphibians - Audubon Society Field Guides, Audubon Society Pocket Guides, Peterson Field Guides, The Birder's Handbook, The Sibley Guide to Birds*